A

WOMEN

LOVE THE

ON

UNBORN, UNLOVED,

LIFE

& NEGLECTED

EDITED BY **TRILLIA NEWBELL**

CONTRIBUTORS

Joy Allmond is a writer/editor for billygraham.org, and has also written for Crosswalk.com, LifeWay, WORLD magazine and the Ethics and Religious Liberty Commission. She lives in Charlotte, N.C., with her husband, Greg, and two almost-grown stepsons, Andrew and Austin.

Kristie Anyabwile is a wife, mom and writer who has contributed to *Word-Filled Women's Ministry* and the *ESV Women's Devotional Bible.* She joyfully supports her husband, Thabiti, as he pastors Anacostia River Church in Washington, D.C. They have three children. You can find her at iamconvinced.wordpress.com and follow her on Twitter at @kanyabwile.

Jennifer Case Cortez is a writer, editor and the mother of four. She and her husband, Daniel, live in Tennessee and serve at Immanuel Church Nashville. Jennifer's writing has been featured on various blogs and in *The Devotional Bible for Dads, The Life Promises Bible* and *The Mom's Bible: God's Wisdom for Mothers.* Being the mother of a child on the autism spectrum has shaped and humbled her in deep and unexpected ways. You can connect with Jennifer at jennifercasecortez.com.

Christina Fox is the author of *A Heart Set Free: A Journey of Hope Through the Psalms of Lament* (2016). She writes for a number of ministry publications and websites, including Desiring God

Ministries. She lives with her husband and two boys in South Florida where she serves in women's ministry at her church. You can find her at christinafox.com.

Cynthia Hopkins has been involved in pro-life work since 1990. Over the years she has held many roles, including director of outreach and executive director at pregnancy centers in both Virginia and Utah. She currently serves as a vice president at Care Net, the nation's largest network of evangelical pregnancy centers. Cindy lives in Fairfax, Va., with her husband of thirty-six years; their favorite past time is spoiling their first and only grandchild, Milo Jeffrey, born in July 2015.

Betsy Childs Howard is an editor for The Gospel Coalition. Her book Seasons of *Waiting: Walking By Faith When Dreams Are Delayed* is forthcoming from Crossway in 2016. She and her husband, Bernard, live in Manhattan.

Krissie Inserra is the former campus coordinator for A Women's Pregnancy Center in Tallahassee, Fla., and she currently volunteers there as a crisis counselor. She is married to Dean Inserra, the founding pastor of City Church Tallahassee. They have three children, Tommy, Ty, and Sally Ashlyn.

Shannon Kotynski is the wife of Donnie and the mother to four energetic boys. Shannon has been trained in leading women's Bible studies through the Simeon Trust Workshop on biblical exposition and has helped lead studies in her church. She and her family currently reside in the Chicago area.

Brittany Lind and her husband, Joel, live in Louisville, Ky., where they are members of Third Avenue Baptist Church. Brittany stays at home with their two children and also writes for The Council on Biblical Manhood and Womanhood. You can read more about their journey with their foster son at lifewiththe-linds.wordpress.com.

Trillia Newbell is the director of community outreach for the Ethics and Religious Liberty Commission. Trillia has a degree in political science from the University of Tennessee, Knoxville, and will be pursuing her M.A. in biblical counseling from The Southern Baptist Theological Seminary. She is the author of two books, *United: Captured by God's Vision for Diversity* and *Fear and Faith*. Trillia lives in the Nashville area with her husband, Thern, and their two children.

Catherine Parks is a co-author of *A Christ-Centered Weddings: Rejoicing in the Gospel on Your Big Day*. She lives with her husband, Erik, and their two children in Nashville, Tenn. You can find her at cathparks.com.

Jackie Hill Perry is a writer and artist. Since being saved from a lifestyle of homosexual sin, Jackie has been compelled to share the light of gospel truth through poetry. Jackie serves as female mentorship coordinator at Grip Outreach for Youth, a non-profit organization loving Chicago's father-less teens. At home, she is known as wife to Preston and mommy to Eden.

Courtney Reissig is a wife, mom and writer. She is the author of *The Accidental Feminist: Restoring Our Delight in God's Good Design*. She lives in Little Rock, Ark., with her husband and three sons. They are members of Midtown Baptist Church, where her husband is one of the pastors.

Kelly M. Rosati is the vice president of community outreach at Focus on the Family where she serves as the ministry spokesperson on Child Advocacy Issues and oversees the Adoption & Orphan Care Initiative, the Sanctity of Human Life department, Option Ultrasound, and the Community Care efforts. She has appeared in the Wall Street Journal, Denver Post, New York Daily News, Christianity Today and numerous radio stations nationwide. She and her husband, John, live with their four children in Colorado Springs.

Lindsay Swartz serves at the Ethics and Religious Liberty Commission as the managing editor of content. She completed her Master of Divinity at The Southern Baptist Theological Seminary. She's navigating single life in her 30s and loves movies, traveling, good food, coffee shops, girly things, being a member at Redemption City Church, and watching sports. She lives in Nashville, Tenn., and is loving every minute of living in Music City.

Candice Watters is a wife, mom and Bible teacher. She is the author of *Get Married: What Women Can Do to Help it Happen*. She and her husband, Steve, coauthored *Start Your Family: Inspiration for Having Babies*. The Watterses live in Louisville, Ky., where they are raising four children. They blog at FamilyMaking.com.

CONTENTS

ON LIFE AND THE FAMILY

ON PROTECTING LIFE

PREMISE

When we think of the word "life," we must begin with the One who created life, sustains life and gives life. Life was God's idea. In the beginning, God created living organisms that would sit at the bottom of the oceans. He created plants that would live and receive sustenance from another creation of his—the sun. And, as the pinnacle of his work, he created male and female, made in his image.

Man would sin, ushering in death, so God sent his son to die on a cross. Jesus' death and resurrection brings eternal life to those who trust in him. Life is important to the Christian because, first and foremost, it is important to God.

Women have a vested interest in the area of life. God created us, in part, to produce and give life to others. Every man and woman walking this earth came about by the means of a woman. Yet it's not only the beginning of life that matters—it's all of life.

Throughout the Scriptures, we see God caring for people in every stage of life and calling Christians to do the same. God cares for those whom society disregards. He cares for the unborn, unloved and neglected. God cares for the orphan, widow, and elderly, for the woman struggling with temptation and sin, for the confused teenage girl, for the one who hurts and the shut-out.

Because all of life is important to God, we are compelled to talk about it. Whether it's addressing purity and teaching our children about sex, teens and pregnancy, caring for the woman with a high-risk pregnancy, children with special needs, caring for the single mother, or getting involved in the pro-life movement, how we interact with God's image-bearers matters.

We cover these topics in *Women on Life*, and it's our desire that this book will inspire you to care deeply about issues of life, equip you for prayerful action and begin a conversation in your churches and homes.

INTRODUCTION

It's funny to think back on the things you said and believed at one point in your life and how sure of yourself you were. I remember a conversation I had with a friend before I became a Christian. I was studying abroad, young and "free". I was self-assured and confident that I was right in the way I processed and viewed the world around me. My friend was a Christian, and although Christians and non-Christians can have similar worldviews, ours couldn't have been more different. I spoke firmly and confidently that to be pro-woman meant to be pro-choice. As a matter of fact, I would have believed that any form of taking control of one's life was completely acceptable (assisted suicide and the like). But with matters of abortion in particular, I was adamant. And I thought I was right.

I grew up believing strongly that every person should have equal rights—every person living and walking was made with the potential to do great things and contribute to society. If you were to label me back then, you'd probably say I was a feminist, pro-choice and politically liberal. Like much of America, I believed that a woman had a right to determine what was best for her body. I believed wholeheartedly that I was also pro-women. No one, I thought, should be allowed to control the outcome of an unwanted pregnancy except for the mother. The male partner didn't have rights to voice an opinion either. I actually don't believe I thought the baby was, in fact, a baby. In other words, I adopted the idea that the life in the womb was a fetus of cells that weren't fully developed, and therefore disposable. There wasn't anything that would have convinced me otherwise.

But God.

Something radical happened to all of my perceived notions of rights when God captured my heart with his gospel. Nothing was the same. As my heart was being transformed, so was my worldview. As I opened the Word, I discovered that what I thought were a bunch of growing, forming cells was actually the created work of God being knit together and molded in a mothers' womb (Psa. 139:13). God wasn't creating a specimen. He was creating a human—a man or woman with incredible worth and made in his image.

Later in life, miscarriages drove home the reality and worth of a life in the womb as I continued to grow in Christ. I got it. I understood that my loss was real. I mourned the deaths of those babies because I knew that children were a heritage from the Lord, the fruit of the womb, a reward (Psa. 127:3). And now that I have two busy and joy-filled children, I understand the joy of a human being that has been born (John 16:21). Oh, what joy!

Lately, as the topic of abortion has reentered the public square with great ferocity, I've found myself weeping, without words and unsure where to begin as I think about discussing the topic with my neighbors. The undercover Planned Parenthood videos have done more than reveal the atrocities associated with abortion; they've ignited a new passion and fire in the hearts of Christians to take up the pro-life cause. There's greater pressure than ever for the government to defund Planned Parenthood, a potential that has felt far-fetched in recent years. Those who were once only slightly engaged with the movement are now fully aware. There's momentum, and we don't want it to stop with Planned Parenthood, but to extend to *all* of life.

Yet, despite the brutality that we've observed, there's still a temptation for Christians to fear and shrink back when expressing dismay over abortion. We may fear speaking the truth—even when speaking the truth in love. We may fear rejection from our liberal-leaning friends. It could be that once the news cycle has turned to the next big thing, we've become apathetic to the seriousness of the situation. Perhaps the hardest accusation that we face is that we aren't pro-women—an accusation that I once used; that being pro-life automatically puts us at odds with what's best for women. These are fears we must wrestle with in order to be empowered to stand for truth, even in the face of adversity.

And just as the saying goes, there's nothing new under the sun. Being pro-life has never been easy. In fact, God gives us a picture of how we can fight our fears and replace them with a better fear through the lives of some Hebrew midwives.

Exodus wastes no time in setting up the scene for the pressures placed on the Israelite people. In Exodus 1-2:10, we get a quick overview of their plight. We are told that the sons of Jacob who first came into Egypt had died, but the people of Israel remained fruitful and increased in number (Exod. 1:5–7). The tides would soon change for Israel, however, as a new king arose over Egypt who didn't know Joseph and the good he had brought. The increasing number of Hebrews was viewed as a threat to Egypt's new king, and as was foretold, the oppression and affliction of Israel would begin.

HEBREW MIDWIVES AND THE FEAR OF THE LORD

Egypt's new king afflicted the people of Israel in every way. They were enslaved and forced to do hard labor, but that still wasn't enough for Pharaoh. He also wanted to ensure their growth would cease—because even with all of the persecution, the Israelites continued to grow in numbers and spread throughout the land (Exod. 1:12). So Pharaoh went after their sons—their babies.

Pharaoh ordered the Hebrew midwives to kill every son born to a Hebrew woman. With what we know in part about what was going on during this time, it would seem that these women would obey the king out of fear for their lives. If Pharaoh had the authority to command them to kill children at birth, he could easily have killed them. But they did not submit to his maniacal plan. Instead, Exodus records, "But the midwives feared God and did not do as the king of Egypt commanded them, but let the male children live" (Exod. 1:17). In the face of persecution, the midwives chose what was right. They chose to fear the Lord and obey him.

So the question is, *can we trust him?* Are we willing to fear him above all earthly powers? Are we committed to his truth enough to stand in faith against the evil that exists in our world today? As we continue to advocate for life, is God worth trusting in the face of ridicule, slander and persecution?

There's a lesson for us to learn from the Hebrew midwives. These women weren't strong and mighty in power—they were strong and mighty in faith. They knew that preserving the lives of these children and disobeying the Pharaoh meant sacrificing their own security. It could have meant their lives, but it didn't matter. They feared God—the God of wrath and judgment, the God of mercy and grace. Are we willing to stand up for what is right like these women, regardless of what it might cost us?

Make no mistake, there's no guarantee that God will keep us from earthly harm, or even death at the hands of Pharaoh. But God does say that those who trust in him are safe (Prov. 29:25)—eternally safe. He reminds us that man can only kill the body, not the soul. Who should we fear then? "But rather fear him who is able to destroy both soul and body in hell" (Matt. 10:28).

At some point, we all must decide whether God is worthy of our trust and admiration. In many ways, we make this choice every day—every minute of the day. But there also may be a situation where, like the Hebrew midwives, you must decide whether to obey the voice of God—the commandments of our Lord—or submit to an authority that is opposed to him. My prayer for you and for me is that by God's grace and power, we'd choose to obey the Lord in supporting mothers, babies, the broken, neglected and overlooked in all of life. Let's ask God to help us fear him above all things, and let's trust him, if he wills, to use our faith to bless many generations to come.

I know many women who've made the choice to abort their baby. I'm aware that some readers who pick up this book will have made that choice. I want them to know—and you to know—that I am pro-women. I don't affirm the past choice to abort, but I believe in a God who hates sin and sent his Son to die on the cross to pay the penalty for our sins. I believe in a God who says that if we confess our sin, he's faithful to forgive us and purify us (1 John 1:9). I believe that all of Romans 8 applies to me and to her and to anyone who has trusted in the Lord.

You, my friend, my sister, are not condemned. That is how I am pro-woman. I want you to know the truth of God's Word and the love found in Jesus. And I want you to know what God thinks about each and every life. He's given every life—no matter how young or old—an incredible gift: we bear his image.

This book is a collection of essays to help us think about life—*all* of life—from the woman who is pregnant and unsure of her next steps, to equipping the church to care for the elderly. We want to be women who love life, and that means caring for the unborn and the born.

PROCEED WITH HOPE

There is an appropriate time for everything, and as we look at the world around us, now is an appropriate time for weeping (Eccl. 3:4). We weep for babies who have lost their lives. We weep for the doctor, nurses and staff who performed abortion procedures. We weep with the hundreds of thousands of mothers who are now weeping because of their decision to abort (some of which are near and dear to my heart). We weep with you, mothers, for the children lost in miscarriage. We weep for the children who have been neglected. We weep for the families separated by death or by rebellion. We weep for the outcast and overlooked.

But we don't mourn as those without hope (1 Thess. 4:13). We can weep with hope knowing that God sent his Son Jesus as a propitiation for our sins, and he will return, vindicating his righteousness. He will make all things new. And we hope in that future grace because we know that his Word is true. Though we are restless and ready for his return, we thank God that he is patient, not wanting anyone to perish (2 Pet. 3:9). We have hope knowing that God's heart also breaks for those he has created. We pray he will use us to make a difference through love, obedience and the work of the Holy Spirit.

ONE

HOLISTICALLY PRO-LIFE

BY TRILLIA NEWBELL

In the beginning, God created. He made the earth, sea, heavens, creatures, and he formed male and female. God did not have to create life. He didn't need humans to inhabit the earth. But he chose to breathe life into our lungs. Don't let the familiarity of this diminish its significance.

Psalm 8:4 begs the question, "What is man that you are mindful of him, and the son of man that you care for him?" and we should all wonder the same. As we know, God is holy and majestic. We agree with the Psalmist throughout chapter 8 that when we look at the heavens and his handiwork, we are perplexed by his love and kindness to sinful man. God's love for mankind cost him his son. Jesus died for those who would believe.

This awareness, an awareness of the love, kindness and goodness toward people—his creation—ignites a different kind of conviction and fire in the Christian heart. If God so loved the world that he gave his only son, then shouldn't we also love the people he created? If Jesus would not discriminate in who he would die for—every tribe, tongue, nation, poor, orphan, men, women and more—shouldn't we be willing to view all men and all of life as immensely valuable?

These are some of the big questions we must wrestle with when considering the pro-life position. Being pro-life is often exclusively linked to being anti-abortion; it isn't less than that, but it's so much more. The pro-life position encompasses that babies are created and important in the womb but also throughout all of life regardless of disabilities (Psa. 139:13). And being pro-life remembers the orphans and widows (Jam. 1:27) and the elderly (Acts 20:35, 1 Tim. 5:1-8). Being pro-life also informs our views on suicide and assisted suicide. To be pro-life is to hold to a belief that all of life matters. Ultimately, being pro-life is to obey the law summed up in two commands: "Love the Lord your God with all your heart and with all your soul and with all your mind. And love your neighbor as yourself" (Matt. 22: 37-40).

I believe there's an interesting example of what Jesus is saying about our love for our neighbor in how we approach social media. The increased use of social media has ushered the word narcissi into our daily language. There isn't a day that goes by that I don't see narcissi referenced. Most people, quite honestly seem to be throwing stones: You are a narcissist if you take a picture of yourself and post it onto social media—also known as a "selfie." You are a narcissist if you post anything about yourself at all. Don't express your feelings because if you do, you are a narcissist.

Although I don't think it's good or right to throw stones and judge others, I do think the naysayers are onto something. Perhaps the missing link is that by nature we are all narcissists. This is why,

I believe, the Lord called us to love others as we love ourselves, because we *do* love ourselves, and we work hard to preserve ourselves. So, of all of the commandments in Deuteronomy and Leviticus, the greatest is that we love our God with all our heart, soul and mind, and love our neighbors as ourselves.

LOVE DOES NO WRONG TO A NEIGHBOR

The gospel is the good news to a dying world. It is the news that saved me as I was walking blindly in my sin and toward eternal damnation. It is the gospel that brings salvation, but God's atoning work on the cross doesn't stop at salvation. Once saved and for as long as I live (here and forevermore), I will be receiving the benefits of Christ's work. And I will also be transformed more and more to his likeness until that day when I am face-to-face with my Savior and the sin that clings so closely is destroyed for good. But until that day, I live among other sinners just like me. Understanding Christ's sacrifice on our behalf affects the way we treat others. Jesus is a friend to sinners and it is by his blood that we can be too. We have a treasure in the gospel and this treasure is what motivates us to preserve life and serve others.

In 1 John, John gives us a call to action based on the work that Christ did on our behalf. He says, "By this we know love, that he laid down his life for us, and we ought to lay down our lives for the brothers" (3:16). Jesus reveals his love for us through the cross. There is no greater evidence of God's abundant love and compassion for us in that he placed his Son on the cross to die on our behalf. And there is no greater love than that which Christ has shown us by absorbing the full fury of his Father's wrath and our sin. Jesus did not fight for his rights to the throne of grace where he rightly belonged. On the contrary, Jesus "in the form of God, did not count equality with God a thing to be grasped, but emptied himself, by taking the form of a servant, being born in the likeness of men" (Phil. 2:6-7). Christ laid down his life for us, and because of his great sacrifice, we should be compelled to lay down our lives for our fellow brothers and sisters in Christ.

Lest we be confused by the call to love our brothers and sisters, God's Word challenges us to love *all* people, even our enemies. This means we love the 90-year-old woman in our congregation, the rambunctious and joyful child with autism, and the hostile non-Christian neighbor struggling with depression. All life matters because all life matters to God. John again challenges us to look to the needs of others, "But if anyone has the world's goods and sees his brother in need, yet closes his heart against him, how does God's love abide in him? Little children, let us not love in word or talk but in deed and in truth" (1 John 3:17-18).

Loving others is one of the many ways we put our faith into action. Like Christ, we die to our own needs, our preferences, and in times of others' needs, our very own bodies and goods to show love and compassion to others. In the Gospel of John, Jesus commands that we love one another just as he has loved us. The sacrificial love on display between Christians is a sign to all people that we are followers of Jesus Christ—by this all will know that we are his disciples (John 13:34-35). This sacrificial love to people who might otherwise be shunned or forgotten is an open invitation of the gospel. We must look to Jesus as our example of love, and we must cling to Jesus for the strength *to* love.

It may seem odd to speak so much of love, but one cannot truly be pro-life without a great love for others. Our lack of compassion for the defenseless and hurting, ignoring the widow and orphan, and forgetting the elderly can be equated to selfishness and self-absorption, which is not love. A holistic pro-life stance is an acknowledgement and adherence to the second commandment. We are to love our neighbors and seek the good of our neighbors—love does no wrong to a neighbor (Rom. 13:10).

So, how do we live out our pro-life convictions? None of us are exempt from the temptation to being pro-life in word but not deed. Practically, our pro-life love for our neighbor is spiritual (through prayer) and tangible (through service). Prayer is not the lesser act. There is power in prayer and it is our means of communicating with our Creator God. We need to pray for the poor, orphan, widow, elderly, disabled and all people. We can ask God to work mightily in our midst and in their lives. We want to pray for national policies to change and the humility of our elected officials.

In addition to prayer, we can take practical steps through teaching what God's Word says about the sanctity of life, and volunteering in the community and with organizations that are equipped to serve the orphans, disabled, pregnant women in crisis, and the elderly. But perhaps the most significant practical thing we can do is to be aware of the needs in our local congregations. We must ask the Lord to give us eyes to see those who are the least of these, those who are struggling with sin and temptation, and those who are alone. We need grace and the power of the Holy Spirit to enable us to put our faith and pro-life convictions into action.[1]

---

1   This chapter will appear in the March 2016 issue of Tabletalk. Ligonier.org/Tabletalk.

TWO

PURSUING PURITY

BY CATHERINE PARKS

Growing up, I could have been the poster child for the purity movement. I signed the pledge card, wore my purity ring—even my name means "pure one." Many high school make-out sessions ended just in time because I had to remain "pure." I knew that if I could just hold out long enough, one day I would no longer have to use restraint, and my husband and I would have amazing sex all the time.

This is my story, but in recent years I have read several similar tales from writers saying this promise of incredible sex in return for waiting until marriage was a lie. These women claim they would have been better off not waiting, and should have gotten experience earlier so they might carry less shame into the wedding night. Because they say the church taught them their desires and bodies were something of which to be ashamed and wary, these feelings were nearly impossible to overcome in marriage.

In many ways, I agree with these writers. Any time the church promises an "if you do this, this good thing will happen to you" scenario, I'm skeptical. In this case, my generation of youth group attendees were told "True Love Waits," and that this "true love" would include great married sex. Many a virgin bride and groom have learned this is not always the case.

Like the fishermen tasked with catching the huge shark in the movie *Jaws* who say, "We're gonna need a bigger boat," the church is realizing our teaching on purity is entirely inadequate. If we are only keeping sex for marriage so that we will have better sex, what hope is that to someone who reaches her forties and is not married? What hope is it to the new believer who has already experienced sex outside of marriage? Or how does this speak to questions about masturbation or pornography?

Recently, I was overseas with my sister-in-law, and we decided to treat ourselves to a little time in an ice café. Literally, the interior of the café was almost completely composed of ice—ice seats, tables, sculptures, igloos, even an ice Transformer statue. The country we were visiting was in the middle of the desert, so this frozen cave was a welcome break from the heat. We sat down to order a drink and decided to try the recommended "Special Hot Chocolate." Turns out their special hot chocolate is just a couple of notches below Swiss Miss. We were craving something warm, and this drink temporarily heated our hands and throats, but the satisfaction was fleeting, and we left with a powdered chocolate taste in our mouths.

A few hours later, we stumbled upon a French café I had visited several years back while in Paris with my husband. Famous for their hot drinking chocolate, my sister-in-law and I couldn't resist stopping in for some. The waiter came with a small pitcher of thick, warm chocolate, and poured it like a gooey waterfall into our teacups. Neither of us could hide our joy at first sip. There really is nothing like it. I sat in silence, wondering how it's possible that someone could capture something so rich and delicious in a simple drink. Even though we were sharing one small pitcher, neither of us could finish it. I hated to leave any of it behind, but one small cup was more satisfying than a lifetime of Swiss Miss.

It would be tempting to tell this story to illustrate the difference between the "Swiss Miss sex" devoid of marital commitment with the beauty and joy of married sex. This is what we have taught people for years, and it has kept a purity ring on many fingers. But I do not believe God meant for good sex to be our ultimate goal in purity. From Eden onward, God shows us he is our ultimate good. Things go awry when we get this wrong.

Paul wrote strong words about impurity in Romans 1:24-27, mentioning mankind's propensity toward "dishonorable passions" and "the dishonoring of their bodies." But this is preceded by these important words from verses 21-23:

> For although they knew God, they did not honor him as God or give thanks to him, but they became futile in their thinking, and their foolish hearts were darkened. Claiming to be wise, they became fools, and exchanged the glory of the immortal God for images resembling mortal man and birds and animals and creeping things.

Paul tells us in verse 24 that it is because of *this* that God gave man up "in the lusts of their hearts to impurity." Because of what? Idolatry. Exchanging the glory of God for the things of earth.

When we place God's good gift of sex on a pedestal, we are

exchanging the beauty and glory of God with a lesser love. Only he truly satisfies.

PURSUING PURITY

So why is purity even important? Why should we not engage in sexual acts outside of marriage? Why did God give us sexuality at all?

When God created woman and brought her to man, man rejoiced because finally, after seeing all God had created, he saw someone like himself. Genesis 2:24 says, "Therefore a man shall leave his father and his mother and hold fast to his wife, and they shall become one flesh. And the man and his wife were both naked and were not ashamed." This picture of the one-flesh union of marriage is given from the beginning of creation, but to what end? Did God create sex solely for the purpose of filling the earth? These verses do not mention procreation, so this cannot be the sole point of sexual union.

If we skip to Ephesians 5, we see Paul reference this verse from Genesis and go on to say, "This mystery is profound, and I am saying that it refers to Christ and the church." Could it be that marriage and the one-flesh union were intended from the beginning to represent a truth about God's relationship *with* us? We were created with a longing for union. Our desire to know and be fully known in relationship with others is a reflection of this. Through Christ, God pursues us, draws us and shows us that, though he knows us fully in all our mess, he loves us fully. There is no fear of rejection, no need to hide in shame. Just as God sacrificed an animal in Eden to cover the shame of Adam and Eve, Christ's sacrifice covers our shame. Through faith in Christ, we can have the ultimate union with him. It is this union that the one-flesh relationship in marriage represents.

Because sex images this union, stripping it of commitment strips it of meaning. Since the sexual revolution of the 70s, women have been trying to figure out how to use sex for their own empowerment. Recent movies depict women engaging in commitment-free sex, unable or unwilling to attach emotional significance to the sexual act out of fear of ruining the enjoyment. But in the end, none of this is truly satisfying. There are articles telling women how to be sure they receive pleasure from hook-ups, and articles lamenting the fact that hooking-up is still predominantly a man's game. And then there are those like pop singer Hailee Steinfeld, whose song "Love Myself" boasts that she doesn't need anyone else to satisfy her, because she can love herself "anytime, day or night." If sexual enjoyment is only about hormones, nerves and endorphins, then why involve anyone else at all?

God never intended for us to find sexual satisfaction from looking at a screen. No man is an island, and those who bear God's image were created for union with him and with one another. Nor did he intend for us to find satisfaction from a physical act separated from total commitment to sharing our lives with another person—till death do us part. In fact, it's actually impossible to do so. Sex is not just "sex." It's an overflow of sacrificial, marital love. It can be perverted within marriage just as it can outside of marriage, but when pursued rightly, it's a selfless act of loving and giving within the safe confines of true commitment.

Dietrich Bonhoeffer wrote about the difference between self-centered love and spiritual love—the kind of pure love only possible through Christ—in his work, *Life Together*:

> Self-centered love loves the other for the sake of itself; spiritual love loves the other for the sake of Christ. That is why self-centered

love seeks direct contact with other persons. It loves them, not as free persons, but as those whom it binds to itself. It wants to do everything it can to win and conquer; it puts pressure on the other person. It desires to be irresistible, to dominate. [. . .] Emotional, self-centered love desires other persons, their company. It wants them to return its love, but it does not serve them. On the contrary, it continues to desire even when it seems to be serving.[1]

Unlike our natural human love, we see true selfless love in Christ, and through Christ we are called and equipped to love in the same way. This Christ-like love means loving one another enough to forsake a physical act that does not go hand-in-hand with marital commitment.

THE STRUGGLE TO WAIT

But what do we do with the desires that still remain? Why did God give us sexual desires if he didn't intend us all to use them?

We see over and over in Scripture that God is a loving God who bestows good gifts on his children (Psa. 84:11, Matt. 7:11). Our sexuality is one of those good gifts. But even the best gifts can become idols. Therefore, we must submit our sexuality to him. Our desire for physical oneness points us to our deepest need for oneness with Christ. Our lack of physical oneness should drive us to seek true satisfaction in him alone. Because he is truly satisfying, we can turn from seeking sexual intimacy outside of his design.

---

1   Bonhoeffer, Dietrich. 2005. *Life Together*, vol. 5 of Dietrich Bonhoeffer Works, English Edition, ed. Geffrey B. Kelly, trans. Daniel W. Bloesch and James H. Burtness. Minneapolis: Fortress Press, p. 42.

We fear giving up sexual autonomy because our culture tells us we're missing out if we aren't hooking up. But Augustine, a fourth century theologian who wrote with beautiful honesty about his conversion to Christianity, gave us these hope-filled words, proclaiming to God, "How sweet all at once it was for me to be rid of those fruitless joys which I had once feared to lose. [. . .] You drove them from me and took their place, you who are sweeter than all pleasure.[2]"

My kids have only ever had Swiss Miss. They do not know the delights of French hot chocolate, so they are content to stir their powdery drink and store-brand marshmallows. But I know that the moment they taste the real thing, they will never want to go back. It's the "expulsive power of a new affection" that theologian Thomas Chalmers[3] preached about.

Life-giving purity will never come from saying, "Do not touch," or, "Do not look." It will only come when impure desires are driven out by something far more satisfying. This is the meaning of sex— that sex isn't about sex at all. It's about God's love for his people. And we can know this love whether we ever experience the one-flesh union or not. Ultimately, he is better. After all, true purity is not found in a pledge, a ring or even abstinence. True purity comes from a heart that has tasted the goodness of the Lord—a good-ness which drives out lesser pleasures.

May we be people who call one another to enjoy the reality of Psalm 34:8: "O, taste and see that the LORD is good!"

---

2   Augustine, Aurelius. Confessions, trans. R. S. Pine-Coffin. New York: Penguin Books, 1961. IX.1.
3   Chalmers, Thomas. *The Expuslive Power of a New Affection*. GLH Publishing, Kindle AZW file.

THREE

SEXUAL SIN, FORGIVENESS, AND THE GOSPEL

AN INTERVIEW WITH JACKIE HILL PERRY

BY TRILLIA NEWBELL

How did you view sex prior to your conversion?

Prior to my conversion, I had two contradicting views on sex. A part of me knew that sex was good and right only when it was expressed in the context of a heterosexual marriage. Having been somewhat exposed to Christian teaching as a young girl, I did not have to be convinced of biblical truth in regards to sex. Yet, this truth did not hold enough weight to prevent me from living out my other view of sex: I believed that only homosexual relations could satisfy me. My inherent depravity and fatherless upbringing led me to look at heterosexual marriage as ideal, but impossible. I found myself physically attracted to men, but emotionally, my heart found more joy in the companionship of a woman. What a tangled mess I was! I had an anxious, conscious warring against a hedonistic heart that only grace could restore.

When you became a Christian, how did this view change?

I was 19 years old when God broke in, overcame my hardness and turned my heart toward him in repentance and faith. My views were not immediately changed, though my nature was. A part of my conversion was recognizing that though homosexual sin was desirable and pleasurable to *me*, this was only the case because of deception. I was deceived into believing that sin could satisfy me more than God—the God that created me for himself, the God that poured his wrath out on his son so that I could experience peace *with* God. By faith in this, along with time in his word and a community of believers, my perspective began to realign. But this didn't mean my struggle didn't continue.

A specific experience that helped root me in truth was during a time of temptation. I might've been a Christian a few years, so temptation was not new, nor were the lies that arose in my heart during those seasons. I was going through a lot emotionally and wanted comfort—not from God or community but from a woman. My desire and the way I wanted comfort from this woman was contrary to the will of God for me. The feelings felt so real, so tangible, so hard to ignore. The Scriptures that condemned the sin of homosexuality were readily available to remind me of the truth, but that meant nothing to me when the truth didn't *feel* true. It meant nothing to me when the truth didn't seem to promise the same immediate comfort and satisfaction that the touch a woman's skin against mine could.

In my desire to resist and flee in the name of faith, I sought God's Word for understanding. God's Word is clear on its position about homoerotic relationships; I wouldn't dare try to convince myself that Leviticus, Romans, and Corinthians were all singing a song of affirmation toward same-sex relationships in order to give room for me to fulfill my lust and destroy my conscience. Though difficult, I believed that the Scriptures were inerrant, inspired, and fully trustworthy, but what I desperately wanted to know was simply *why*. Why was my desire to be with a woman wrong?

I went back to the beginning, to Genesis. I wanted to understand God's heart as much as I understood his commands. There, I saw God's character as a wise, loving, and authoritative Creator who had clear intentions for his creations. Sexuality was his, created by him, and for his glory. And this sexuality was created to function between a man and woman—both made with distinctions that made them one. God declared all of this *good*. When sin entered in, humanity became false judges of what is good and good *for* them. And I got it! In my temptations, I needed to recognize that God condemns homosexuality because he knows what is good for his glory and good for me. Holy sexuality would only be lived out with joy when my perspective aligned with the truth that God was ultimately wiser than me.

It seems that, though we are talking more frequently about sexual temptation and sin among women, it's still slightly taboo. How can we encourage women to be open in this area?

Shame has made women less likely to discuss sexual sin and temptation among themselves. Shame has led many to isolate themselves from community. Wives don't feel they have the freedom to confess to their husbands. This shame has driven women to not only hide from themselves but also from God. Shame has a sense of pity attached to it, but there are lies beneath that involve fear and pride. Fear of man and pride leads women to be more concerned about how they may be perceived by people and less about how God sees them in Christ. We will only become open as women when discussing sexual sin when we begin to walk in humility. Humility must be displayed through confession of temptations and sin and from the community where these confessions will most likely take place.

This humility is first vertical, humbled under God and completely aware of how he sees us; it understands he is completely omniscient and yet we are completely accepted in Christ, made righteous by faith in him (Rom. 3:21-26). If the truth of our standing with God anchors us, then we have no need to hide before men. Their acceptance or rejection does not change our identity—nor does the temptation or the sin we struggle against change our standing with God. Therefore, we are free to be open without shame, thus making our humility horizontal.

I would argue that this is even more crucial as a community of women. A woman can be free in her heart but can become guarded and closed due to a community of women who have yet to become free themselves. When the women in our local churches all recognize the love and acceptance they have in Christ as individuals, they will become bearers of love and grace toward the women around them, creating a community built on love, freedom, and honesty.

There can be a temptation for the woman struggling with sexual sin to place her identity in her temptation. How do we encourage Christian women to find their identity in Christ?

The woman who is struggling to find her identity in Christ is the woman who is struggling to believe the Word of God. If we are to encourage women to see themselves as Christ sees them, the fuel of our exhortation must be completely founded in the Scriptures. One of the aspects of our fallen humanity is that we are easily swayed by the opinions of others, including ourselves. We define our physical beauty by compliments, or the lack thereof. We are attracted to people, jobs, or clothing not merely because of the things themselves, but because of the false identity they give us. The temptation to find our identity outside of Christ still exists *in* Christ, but God is faithful to consistently point us to truth that comes from Word of God.

God has some things to say about us that should completely revolutionize how we see ourselves. For example, we are called "new creatures" (2 Cor. 5:17), children of God (1 John 10:12) , hidden with Christ in God (Col. 3:3), heirs with Christ (Rom. 8:17), and God's workmanship (Eph. 2:10). What God has to say about us must outweigh how we (or others) see ourselves, but this will not happen unless we believe God by believing his Word.

So, if we have a heart to encourage women who are struggling to find their identity in Christ, we must help them grow in faith. They must come to grips with their unbelief and how it can permeate all that they are—so much so that it leads them to search high and low to find their identity from things and people in whose image they aren't even created. Help the women around you trust God's Word more, and you will see them content with what God says about them.

How does the gospel help us think through this temptation and sin as we struggle in this area?

Many have employed moralistic tactics to defeat sin in hopes of attaining the victory they desire. Meanwhile the gospel of Jesus Christ has won the battle already! One thing about the gospel that encourages me in the war against sin and the temptations that proceed it is this: when Christ died, after taking on the penalty of my sin, he was buried. The grave did not and could not hold him for too long because he is God. As a result, Christ rose from the grave with all power in his hand, defeating death and sin once and for all. For whom did he do this? For those who repent and believe in him. Romans 6:5-11 says this:

> For if we have been united with him in a death like his, we shall certainly be united with him in a resurrection like his. We know that our old self was crucified with him in order that the body of sin might be brought to nothing, so that we would no longer be enslaved to sin. For one who has died has been set free from sin. Now if we have died with Christ, we believe that we will also live with him. We know that Christ, being raised from the dead, will never die again; death no longer has dominion over him. *For the death he died he died to sin, once for all, but the life he lives he lives to God. So you also must consider yourselves dead to sin and alive to God in Christ Jesus.*

For the believer struggling with sin and temptation, whether it is homosexuality or the like, when Christ died to sin, *you* died to sin. Because Christ rose from the dead, *you* also share in his resurrection. The good news of Jesus gives us a completely new perspective on sin. Sin has a way of making us feel like victims, like a tragedy waiting to happen. But the gospel tells us that the sin that seems so near has no power over us. We don't have to give in, we don't have to submit, we don't have to be discouraged or defeated because Christ is no longer in the grave. And if Christ has been raised, then we have too!

How does the gospel help us think through this temptation and sin as those who disciple others who struggle in this area?

In our hope to disciple those who struggle in the area of homosexuality, we should make sure to actually define what we mean by struggle. Some may be far from struggling and are still slaves to sin. Others may be set free from sin but still fighting against it by the power of God's Spirit. Both need the gospel shared from believers in their lives. But how the gospel applies to each is nuanced. For the unbeliever, we must reiterate the truth of God's character—holiness, kindness, justice, mercy—and how they, as a sinner, have rebelled against the one they were made to worship, not just because they have acted out on their same-sex attraction, but because they are born in sin. The gospel does not isolate sin from its root. The people we are hoping to lead in truth are not just "homosexual people." They are not projects to be fixed; they are people to be loved. For the believer with same-sex attraction, they are just as needy of the gospel as the unbeliever. We cannot assume that the believer is exempt from needing to hear and be reminded of the gospel. They must hear of God's character and Christ's life, death, and resurrection. In light of sin and temptation, both the unbeliever and believer need the hope of the gospel.

Our culture is speaking a language of hopeless under the guise of "being born that way." The claim is that someone with same-sex attraction cannot change, but the gospel says otherwise. In Paul's letter to the Corinthians, he speaks of sinners that will shut many out of the kingdom of heaven, such as drunkards, adulterers, sexually immoral people, *and* homosexuals. This condemnation is bleak and sad if left there. But Paul is full of gospel truth, completely aware of how Christ takes sinners and makes them saints—not only in identity, but nature. He is aware of a gospel so miraculous that it literally *changes* people, giving them the power to flee all that they were once slaves to and giving them the desire to cling to something better, primarily God, himself.

It seems as if Paul was writing to people who, now believers in this miraculous gospel, were once slaves to the exact same sins that will merit eternal damnation. We know this because he goes on to say, "And such were some of you. But you were washed, you were sanctified, you were justified in the name of the Lord Jesus Christ and by the Spirit of our God" (1 Cor. 6:10). With that in mind, our approach to those we disciple has to be one full of gospel-centric hope. The gospel we preach and live by is the gospel that converts *and* sanctifies all who believe it to be true. Homosexuality is not the final verdict for someone captured by the good news, so may the gospel stay in our heart, radiate in our life, and forever be in our mouths.

FOUR

INSTRUCTING KIDS IN THE TRUTH ABOUT SEX

BY CANDICE WATTERS

Some kids used to grow up on farms watching animals reproduce. Parents still had to help them connect the dots between what they were seeing in the barn yard and what would one day happen in the bedroom, but it was a more organic learning process. Surely it was easier to talk to kids about sex. You could just quote Job 12:7.

"Mom, what's sex?"

"Oh honey, I'm busy threshing the grain, why don't you go ask the beasts, and they will teach you; the birds of the heavens, and they will tell you!"

We're mostly removed from the natural setting of the farm, but that's not the reason these conversations are difficult for parents. And the difficulty isn't a modern-day problem. Ever since man left Eden, everything about sex—including how we tell our children about it—has gotten complicated. What happened?

God made sex good (Gen. 1:26-28, 31; 2:18-25). He created the unashamed nakedness between husband and wife that leads to human flourishing, as well as the fruitfulness he commands. But Adam and Eve were unashamed *before* the fall. Sin changed everything. Because of the shame introduced by sin, we tend to avoid talking about sex for as long as possible, and when it's unavoidable, we stumble around not knowing what to say or mimic the crude understanding of the culture.

If we mumble or stay silent, we leave our kids to find out what they can on their own. In our hyper-sexualized culture, that's bad enough. But what's worse is that if our children misunderstand sex, they will misunderstand the gospel.

Much is at stake. So where should you begin?

TRUST GOD'S WORD

I didn't always feel prepared to talk about sex with our kids. Once, I emailed our pastor the week before he was planning to preach on Proverbs 5, the adultery chapter, to ask if it would be "safe for the whole family." I needed Mr. Beaver's rebuke, "Who said anything about safe? 'Course he isn't safe. But he's good. He's the King, I tell you."[1]

---

1   C.S. Lewis, *The Lion, the Witch and the Wardrobe.* (Geoffrey Bless, 1950). Copyright by C. S. Lewis Pte. Ltd.

God created sex. He is the King, he is good, and he has told us in his Word what we need to know about sex in its goodness, as well as its brokenness. Since joining a biblically faithful church that preaches the whole counsel of Scripture, I have learned to trust God's Word. He has given us everything we need for life and godliness (2 Pet. 1:3). That includes instruction about things that make us uncomfortable. And not incidentally, it reveals the reason for our discomfort. We must think about sex—created, fallen and redeemed—as we prepare to teach our children about it.

SEX IS FROM GOD

The Bible talks about sex: the creation of sex, the purpose of sex, the limits on sex and the typology of sex. Sex was God's idea, given to us in marriage for the procreation of children, for a remedy against sin, and for the mutual delight of husband and wife, to paraphrase the *Book of Common Prayer*. It is an earthy, physical gift that employs all the human senses. It is also a sign pointing to something eternal. Ephesians 5:31-32 says,

> "'Therefore a man shall leave his father and mother and hold fast to his wife, and the two shall become one flesh.' This mystery is profound, and I am saying that it refers to Christ and the church."

There is only one type of sex that does this—sex between a man and a woman within the protective covenant of marriage. And Scripture is clear that all manner of sex outside of how God intends it is forbidden. Why so much emphasis in the Bible on how not to have sex? Because as creatures made in God's image, we tend, in our fallenness, to try and remake sex in our own image, according to our sinful desires.

SEX IS EASILY MISUSED

We need to tell our children that sex is easily misused. They will *want* to disobey God's rules about sex; maybe not today, maybe not for a while, but the temptation will come. We have a known and strong enemy, and he is bent on devouring your children (1 Pet. 5:8). Parents, do not think that if you never mention sexual deviancy that your children will never learn of it. The culture we live in is sexually oversaturated. They *will* hear. They *will* see. But even if they are deaf and blind, they have within them their greatest enemy:

> The heart is deceitful above all things, and desperately sick; who can understand it? (Jer. 17:9).

> For from within, out of the heart of man, come evil thoughts, sexual immorality, theft, murder, adultery (Mark 7:21).

Further, Scripture shows that when we do have sex according to our liking with no regard for God's design, we face the consequences.

CHRIST IS OUR HOPE FOR RIGHTLY ENJOYED SEX

But we are not without hope. Sexual union in marriage points us back to the gospel. If you find this hard to comprehend, that's good. God tells us it is a "profound mystery." We are not meant to fully understand it, but to receive it. Because the one-flesh union of marriage points to Christ and the church, we are to honor what sex points to by honoring the limits God has placed on sex. Also, we can take great comfort in the fact that sex is not the ultimate goal. Rightly enjoyed, sex points to the very reality that can set us free from sexual brokenness. It is the good news of Christ crucified, risen and ascended that offers us hope for redemption.

HOW TO SPEAK OF THIS MYSTERY

What does it look like to speak thoughtfully and faithfully about sex? In some ways, it will be like any other conversation. But in other important ways, it will be set apart. Sex is earthy and entirely natural, but it is not prosaic or commonplace. Conversations about sex should be approached in the fear of the Lord, with awe and wonder, even when you're talking while setting the table and peeling potatoes for dinner.

Welcome your children's questions about everything so they'll come to you about this. If they're in the habit of talking to you because you create a culture of conversation in your family, then the opportunities to talk about sex should arise naturally. You want them to feel comfortable asking you about sex! Turn off your electronic devices (and theirs) so when you walk along the way or drive along the carpool route, they are not distracted by their iPods and DVD players.

How can you speak about something that is at once down-to-earth and sacred? How can you overcome feeling nervous, inadequate, and uncomfortable?

Tell the truth. When they ask, tell the truth. Use anatomical terms, not slang. That doesn't mean you must teach them every word and biological reality all at once. The Bible uses metaphor and poetry in many of its discussion of sex. But the Bible uses the language of the garden, not the gutter. We should do the same.

Keep your answers appropriate to their age and maturity. You must tell them the truth in everything, but you need not tell them everything at the first curious question. There is a range of honest, helpful answers to the question, "Where do babies come from?" Even as I was answering one of our son's early questions about sex—explaining the basics of how God created male and female bodies to fit together—I was realizing how much more there is yet to tell. He is only beginning to learn. This is a progressive unfolding that should match his growth and development.

Don't overwhelm them. Some precocious children will ask for more than they're ready to handle. What then? It's OK to say, "We'll keep talking, and over time, we'll fill in more details. Some things would feel like a burden too heavy for you to carry right now." For example, when one of our young sons asked, while looking at his assortment of Scrabble tiles, if r-a-p-e is a word, I answered simply, "Yes, it is a word. But no, you may not use that word because it describes a horrible violence by men using their physical strength against women." That was enough for him to know that day.

The goal is to equip your children with knowledge, not burden them with it.

When something happens, talk about it. When you walk past the magazine rack at the store, an ad pops up on your laptop, the check-out clerk is dressed immodestly—whatever it is, when you think your children have seen or heard something potentially sexual, raise the issue. Don't wait for them to say something; likely they won't. When you get back to the car, initiate a conscience-forming conversation.

If your kids are young, it might sound like this,

"Kids, I'm sorry that we just saw something that is dishonoring to the Lord. When a woman dresses immodestly, it draws attention to her body in inappropriate ways. You know the Bible says 'we are bought with a price, so glorify God with your body.' Let's pray for her."

Then lead your kids in a prayer for the woman they saw. Ask God to show her what it means to steward the gift of a physical body for the good of others and the glory of God. Ask him to guard your children from the desire to use his gifts in ways that he doesn't intend. Ask him to help you all conduct yourselves like Jesus did, with humility and modesty.

When your six, seven or eight year old starts putting two and two together after volunteering with you at the Crisis Pregnancy Center, you might say,

"You'll learn more about this as you get older, but for now it's enough to know that God's good plan for having babies is with a Mommy and a Daddy who are married. Every life is a miracle, but it is possible to disobey God's plan. We want to help you obey. The tragedy of a baby without a daddy is not the baby, but the disobedience. Disobedience separates us from God. We must always strive to obey God's good design. He is for us and his plans lead to our flourishing!"

If your kids are older and you know you're about to enter a potentially tempting situation, you can give them a heads-up that you're praying for them. Encourage them not to look at another person lustfully; to obey Jesus' call to be pure in heart so that they might see God (Matt. 5:8).

Don't get hijacked. If your child comes to you saying she overhead such and such on the bus or learned this or that from the kid next door, don't panic. It's easy to feel like all your well-crafted plans for a gospel-centered discussion have been ruined, but you don't have to be hijacked by the kids on the school bus. God is sovereign over everything that happens, including the timing and substance of this conversation. Take a deep breath, and take responsibility. Answer your child's questions, and ask a few of your own. Find out what she's heard, and correct any misinformation. Fill in the gaps, and point her to the truth.

Learning about sex is not a one-time event. Part of what kids need to learn is that there is a lot of misinformation out there. We are meant to have many conversations. Some will be prompted by what our kids overhear or see.

Drop everything I've seen God use such moments to lead to a discussion that needed to happen; one that I may have been forgetting or neglecting to have. The timing or setting may not seem ideal, but don't miss the opportunity. Sometimes you have to change your plans, find a quiet, discrete setting, and have *the conversation* right now. Trust God, and seize the moment.

Pray for discernment. How much to say? What words to use? When to bring something up? When to end the conversation and go back to what you were doing? The Lord knows what is best for your children. Ask him to fill you with wisdom (Jam. 1:5). Ask him to make you discerning and to help you pay attention to what's on your kids' minds. Ask the Spirit to prompt you to speak when you should. He is faithful. He will surely do it.

"Mom, what's sex?"

That's the question I heard matter-of-factly, full voice, at the end of a chapel service we were attending together as a family. The sermon text was Hebrews 12:1-17, and the preacher had spent one of his three points on verses 16-17,

> See to it that no one fails to obtain the grace of God; that no 'root of bitterness' springs up and causes trouble, and by it many become defiled; that no one is sexually immoral or unholy like Esau, who sold his birthright for a single meal.

Our eight-year-old son was doing what he always did when he heard a word he didn't understand: he asked me what it meant. He had heard *sex* in other sermons and conversations with our older kids, but this time he was listening. I was glad the question came to me. I had been praying about this conversation, and by God's grace, I was ready to answer.

ON THE BEGINNING OF LIFE

FIVE

WALKING WITH WOMEN THROUGH A HIGH-RISK PREGNANCY

BY COURTNEY REISSIG

I have a rough relationship with pregnancy. I've seen that second pink line show up four times now, yet I only have three children here with me (two of them are twins). My first pregnancy was my "least complicated" even though it ended in miscarriage. It was a textbook case, really. Spotting at six and a half weeks, an ultrasound confirming no heartbeat, and the emotional aftermath of a lost baby. But it was nothing compared to my other three pregnancies. It took us two more years to see that second pink line again, but at our first ultrasound for our second pregnancy, we heard the surprising words—"there are two heartbeats." We were praying for a healthy baby, and in God's kindness, we got two.

And so began my journey with complicated pregnancies.

A twin pregnancy is much different than a singleton pregnancy. Depending on the type of twins (identical or fraternal), a mom may spend a lot of time in the doctor's office with routine ultrasounds, especially toward the end of her pregnancy. My twins are identical and were classified as the second most high-risk because they shared a placenta. The risks that surround a shared placenta pregnancy can be scary if you read too much. And I felt all of that fear.

At two days shy of 32 weeks, my fears were realized when we were told that Baby A was no longer safe inside me. Baby B was taking all his nutrients. My first experience with a live birth was chaotic, unexpected and eerily silent as we waited for our premature babies to take their first labored breaths. Five long weeks in the NICU later, our babies came home, tiny and healthy.

My third pregnancy was a complicated miscarriage that lasted longer than my doctor expected and ended in a Dilation and Curettage (a procedure to remove the baby) weeks later. My fourth pregnancy—far less complicated by my standards— was still filled with less-than-routine issues and a sudden and scary delivery.

With all of my pregnancies, my doctor has said to me, "There are some risks involved, but usually those complications are rare." And on more than one occasion my doctor has also said to me, "You seem to be the exception to the rule."

Maybe you can relate. Or maybe you are a pastor or church leader who wants to love someone well through a complicated pregnancy. Regardless, complicated pregnancies happen and are difficult to walk through alone.

A LABOR OF LOVE

Having a baby for any woman is hard work. It takes its toll on your body and your mind. In a culture that sees any invasion of our personal autonomy as something to be avoided, pregnancy is one of the lasting things that women keep doing even when it is fraught with risks and pain.

But how do you serve a woman (and her family) when pregnancy isn't going according to plan? How do you serve her when she doesn't fit the textbook definition of how a person gets pregnant, carries a child and delivers that child? As pro-life Christians, we rejoice when a friend announces her pregnancy on social media, we throw showers for a friend who is expecting another baby, we even pray outside abortion clinics.

Yet, how do we respond when our friend has to go to the doctor for regular ultrasounds every week? How do we respond when our friend tells us her baby has little chance for a normal life outside of the womb or no chance for life outside the womb? Do we grieve? Do we walk the hard, long road that a high-risk pregnancy entails? I want to suggest some ways we can love and serve someone in a high-risk pregnancy.

EVERYONE IS DIFFERENT

Before I get into any practical counsel, I want to mention that everyone is different. What works for one woman won't work for another. Some women need a healthy dose of reality when you talk to them, while some need a listening ear. My husband regularly says that people are complex and situations are complex. This is true in a high-risk pregnancy. Any counsel I provide must be weighed with this in view. Know your friend. Know your church member. Ask them questions about their baby.

High-risk pregnancies are labeled this way for a number of reasons. Sometimes it is because a woman has had multiple miscarriages and is under observation to prevent any additional miscarriages. Sometimes it is because she is carrying multiples (twins, triplets or more). Sometimes her age makes her high-risk, or a pre-diagnosed disease or physical ailment. Sometimes the baby she is carrying is sick and in need of constant monitoring.

There are a host of reasons why a woman could be labeled high-risk, so knowing that reason and knowing her disposition will go a long way in serving her as she carries her baby to term. It may be her first time being pregnant, or she may have walked this road multiple times before with no baby to hold at the end of it. Each experience will shape her response to being high-risk.

UNDERSTAND THE CURSE

With a high-risk pregnancy comes the realization that we live in a post-Genesis 3 world. When sin came on the scene, everything that God created was affected. What God designed to bring joy is now laced with sorrow. This applies to all aspects of motherhood, but we see it clearly in how broken bringing children into the world can be. In an increasingly pro-natural childbirth culture where we celebrate all that a woman's body can do (and it truly is amazing), we can often forget that there are many women weeping over what their body can't do. Birth, whether natural or not, is still painful (Gen. 3:16). A high-risk pregnancy is a unique reminder that all is not right in the world. It is a reminder that death, sorrow and sickness still have a foothold in this sin-cursed world. It stings the high-risk mother acutely.

KNOW HER BABY

For the pregnant mother whose baby is sick, it can be especially painful to watch other mothers walk through pregnancy unscathed. If her baby is not expected to have a normal life or live past birth, every healthy baby is a reminder of what she will not have with this baby inside of her. One practical way you can walk with her through this sorrow is to know the baby she is carrying. Ask her questions about the baby and his or her development. Offer to drive her to doctor's appointments or do her grocery shopping. Her every waking moment will likely be spent wondering and worrying about her unborn baby. Honoring the life of her baby, no matter how long it lasts, can breathe life into her breaking heart.

FIGHT THE MOMMY WARS
WITH A BETTER WEAPON

The mommy wars are alive and well in the pregnancy world, as you are probably aware. The battle begins before that first wave of morning sickness. But what works in a normal pregnancy might not work in a high-risk pregnancy. If she's on bed rest, she won't be able to decorate the nursery. If her baby is born early, she may not have time to stock up on diapers or wash all of the baby clothes in Dreft. If she is sick and unable to nurse, she may feel the sting of the constant refrain that "breast is best." If her baby has special needs, developmental therapy sessions will likely replace play dates.

While the mommy wars rage around us, we have a better weapon for the high-risk mommas in our lives. Gloria Furman says this about the mommy wars:

> So-called mommy wars have no place among Christian sisters. Christian mothers are weak and needy for one another. Like the faithful Canaanite mother, we approach the Savior on our knees, saying, "Lord, help me" (Matt. 15:21-28). That is the posture of the needy, Christian mother.[1]

A mom in a high-risk pregnancy knows her weakness. She feels her desperate need with every swift kick from her baby and every needle poke from her doctor. Instead of heaping the world's advice on her weary soul, heap Christ on her soul instead. Give her the healing balm of Christ's care for her life and her baby's life. Take her to the Savior who knows what it means to suffer a seemingly senseless death, who understands loss and pain personally, and can sympathize with us in our weakness (Heb. 4:15). The Christ who defeats our enemies also puts the mommy wars to bed with his perfect and finished work (1 Cor. 15:25).

A WORD TO THE SCARED PREGNANT MOMMAS

Before I conclude, I would like to speak to the mommas in high-risk pregnancies. I know you are scared. I know you wake every morning with a lot of uncertainty and voices telling you what to do

---

1   "Mommy Wars in the Local Church: A Parable," by Gloria Furman, *Mom Enough: The Fearless Mother's Heart and Hope*, edited by Tony and Karalee Reinke, Desiring God: 2014, 49.

with that uncertainty. I've been there. I've been in ultrasound rooms and heard the words, "I'm sorry there is no heartbeat." I've been in an operating room staring at the faces of my premature babies, praying they would just take a breath. I've held my tiny baby's hand while he was attached to way too many wires, and I've grieved over babies I've never held.

Pregnancy is fear inducing for me. It's also incredibly disappointing. There are a lot of emotions that can rise within us when we are faced with a pregnancy that is risky or unique. You may feel bitterness that you are walking this road instead of the pregnant woman sitting next to you at the doctor's office. You may be tempted to doubt God's goodness. You may be driven to despair when you read the information provided to you about your baby and his or her needs. You may resent the fact that you are pregnant at all—it's simply not what you expected it to be.

Fear is probably the emotion that rules them all.

But you are brave, sister. Braver than you know. With every day you carry that baby, you are telling a lost world that life matters. You are a walking testimony to the value of life. Your willingness to give yourself physically for your baby, a baby who needs you desperately, is beautiful in God's eyes. He sees. He knows you and loves your baby. Your life is not forgotten to him. Your baby's life is not forgotten to him.

The baby you carry was formed by the God who is sustaining all things by his very word (Col. 1:17, Heb. 1:3). You can trust him. In your exhausted fear you can rest in his goodness, in his care for you, and in his sovereign plan for your life. I say this as a woman who has been on the receiving end of hard news on more than one occasion: he will not leave you or forsake you (Deut. 31:6).

Walking with a woman through a high-risk pregnancy can be all-consuming. It won't always look like the social media-inspired pregnancies and baby stuff we consume on a regular basis. For some, it will be emotional and exhausting. For others, it will be sorrowful and bleak. But it will always be worth it.

The world tells us that babies who are frail, babies who are sick, babies who don't stand a chance, aren't worth celebrating, aren't worth saving, and aren't worth acknowledging. But we know a better answer. Loving a woman in a high-risk pregnancy tells a confused world that life matters, that every baby is a treasure, and that even the sickest and neediest among us deserve our care. The world is not worthy of them or their mommas (Heb. 11:38).

SIX

TEENS, PREGNANCY AND THE FAMILY

BY CHRISTINA FOX

When you hear that a teen in your church is pregnant, what are some of the first thoughts that come to your mind? Do you shake your head and think, "She's ruined her life." Or maybe, "Doesn't she know better?" Perhaps you wonder what went wrong in her family; maybe her parents gave her too much freedom.

We all have responses to the news of a teen pregnancy. I remember one friend's response after we heard about a teen we both knew who had gotten pregnant. She said to me, "This is an amazing opportunity for God's grace to work in their family." I've never forgotten this response because it's not typical. We don't usually think of God's grace when we think about teen pregnancy.

But the truth is, God's grace is always at work, even in difficult and challenging circumstances. His grace is available to parents as we raise children in a sex-saturated culture. It is also available to our children as they face sexual temptation. And above all, it is there for the teen who finds herself pregnant.

THE PROBLEM

The statistics for teen pregnancy tell us that, nationwide, teen pregnancy has dropped in recent years. In 2013, about 273 thousand babies were born to teens ages 15-19. This is a 10 percent drop from the year before.[1] While this is good news, the question is, does that mean teens are not as sexually active as in the past?

The CDC reports that in a 2013 survey of high school students, 46 percent had engaged in sexual activity before. Nearly half of the 20 million new cases of STD's are found in those ages 15-24.[2] The CDC also reports that 90 percent of sexually active teens reported using some form of birth control.[3]

While there has been a reduction in teen pregnancy in recent years, the U.S. still has more teenage pregnancies than other developed countries. And as we see, teens are sexually active. While teenage pregnancy is a huge concern, it only points to a greater problem: teen sexual activity.

---

1   Centers for Disease Control. *Reproductive Health: Teen Pregnancy http://www.cdc.gov/teenpregnancy/about/index.htm* (accessed 10/10/15)
2   Centers for Disease Control. *Sexual Risk Behaviors: HIV, STD, & Teen Pregnancy Prevention http://www.cdc.gov/healthyyouth/sexualbehaviors/* (accessed 10/10/15)
3   Centers for Disease Control. *Few Teens Use the Most Effective Types of Birth Control http://www.cdc.gov/media/releases/2015/p0407-teen-pregnancy.html* (accessed 10/10/15)

Before we can address the issue of teen pregnancy and helping our children navigate the challenges of our culture, we need to see how teen pregnancy fits into the big picture and God's response to it. To do that, we have to return to the beginning.

IN THE BEGINNING

When God spoke the world into being, he said it was good. When he brought forth trees, plants, animals and fish, he said it was good. After making man, he looked at all he had made and said it was very good (Gen. 1:31).

Scripture tells us that God created Adam and Eve as image bearers. "Then God said, 'Let us make man in our image, after our likeness. And let them have dominion over the fish of the sea and over the birds of the heavens and over the livestock and over all the earth and over every creeping thing that creeps on the earth'" (Gen. 1:26). Unlike all the other creatures God made, mankind would be thinking, feeling, creating and governing beings. And also unlike other creatures, Adam and Eve had a friendship with God.

Adam was created first. God said it wasn't good for Adam to be alone and created Eve out of a rib in his side. When Adam first met Eve he said, "'This at last is bone of my bones and flesh of my flesh; she shall be called Woman, because she was taken out of Man.' Therefore a man shall leave his father and his mother and hold fast to his wife, and they shall become one flesh" (Gen. 2:23-24). God commanded them to be fruitful and multiply and fill the earth.

God is the inventor of sex. It was his idea. But he created it with special instructions. It is to be enjoyed within the bond of marriage between one man and one woman. Its purpose it to provide joy and intimacy between the husband and wife (see the Song of Solomon), create new life (Gen. 2:24) and point others to Christ and his bride, the church (Eph. 5:22-33).

But as we know, Adam and Eve disobeyed God's command to not eat of the tree in the middle of the Garden (Gen. 3). They sinned, and in so doing, brought sin into the world. As a result, we are all born into sin (Rom. 3:23). This means that not only do we commit sins, we *are* sinners.

Sin has marred and permeated all that God has made, including his design for sex. Now, people follow their desires instead of God's plan and pursue sexual relationships outside of marriage (Rom. 3:24-27). The world is filled with stories of God's design for sex being broken in a myriad of ways including pornography, adultery, homosexuality, incest and rape. When a teen steps outside of God's design and has sex, pregnancy is one natural consequence, as well as STDs and broken relationships. The sin of sex outside of marriage can also multiply into other sins, such as abortion.

This is the world in which we live. It is the world in which our children live. And we need to understand the origins of the problem before we can begin to know how to face it.

REDEMPTION OF SIN

The story of creation describes God's plan for us, the fall tells us what happened and how we got to where we are, and the story of redemption shows us that God's grace has cut into this fallen world and brought redemption, hope and healing.

After Adam and Eve fell into sin, God promised a Savior in

Genesis 3:15. The rest of the Old Testament reveals the need for this Savior, foretells of who this Savior would be, and pushes forward the plan for his arrival. In the New Testament we meet the Savior, Jesus Christ. He came in the most surprising of ways, through the womb of an unwed teen. As the angel explained to Mary, "'The Holy Spirit will come upon you, and the power of the Most High will overshadow you; therefore the child to be borne will be called holy—the Son of God'" (Luke 1:35).

When he was 30 years old, Jesus began to teach about God's kingdom. He gathered a ragtag group of disciples and traveled around the region teaching, healing and delivering people from their bondage. He revealed the heart and intent of God's law, showing that sin isn't only what someone does, but it is also what someone thinks. He taught that all sin, including sexual sin, begins in the heart, "But I say to you that everyone who looks at a woman with lustful intent has already committed adultery with her in his heart" (Matt. 5:28).

In John 4, Jesus met a Samaritan woman at the well. As Jesus spoke to her about a mysterious source of water, he revealed that he knew more about her than she knew about herself. He knew about her multiple husbands and the sinful life she led. But he offered her more. He offered her grace and water that could quench the thirst that no man could ever quench. She ran off to the village, telling everyone about the grace of Christ, "Come, see a man who told me all that I ever did. Can this be the Christ?" (John 4:29).

When he had completed his ministry, Jesus went like a lamb to the slaughter. Though he was perfect and had never sinned, he laid down his life to free us from all our sin. Through faith in

Christ, we have been set free from the bondage of sin and are freed to live for him.

This is the grace that our children and our teens need to know. Without this grace, we cannot hope to follow and obey Christ in a fallen world, especially in a world broken with sexual sin.

How can God's grace guide us in talking about sexuality with our children or in dealing with the problem of teen pregnancy? How can God's grace walk with us through the news that a teen in our church is pregnant?

OUR CHILDREN

As parents, it is our responsibility to teach and train our children in the Lord (Deut. 6:5-9). We are the primary conduits of God's grace, telling our children the good news of Christ and what he has done through his perfect life, sacrificial death and glorious resurrection.

Part of that responsibility includes teaching our children God's design for them. They need to know what it means to be made in the image of God. They need to know what it means to be a girl or boy and what it looks like to be a godly man or woman. And they need to know God's perfect design for sex.

We need to teach our children God's design for sexuality at an early age. We can start simple and add more information as they mature. When they are young, we draw the outline of the picture and as they grow, we fill in the details. Author David White explains, "Too many parents wait for that one-time, preteen, gut-wrenching conversation. But if you wait until your child is 10 to 12 years old to talk about sex, they will likely have already learned it from another source . . . Ideally, rather than a single, dreaded ordeal, sexual conversations should begin early and continue throughout the child's life."[4]

Our children need this information long before they are teens and are tempted to step outside God's plan for their lives. In starting these conversations early, talking about sexuality becomes a normal course of conversation between parent and child. The more a child is used to talking openly with their parents about how God made them, the more likely they will turn to their parents with questions in the future.

There are a number of useful resources for Christian parents to use in instructing children about sexuality from a biblical perspective. Seek out such resources. Ask fellow church members what they have used. Be prepared before your children ask questions. But even if your children are nearing adolescence and you haven't yet taught them about God's design, it's never too late to start.

OUR TEENS

When I was a teen, scare tactics were often employed by youth groups to convince teens not to have sex. We were shown horrifying images of STD's and reminded of the risks of teen pregnancy. For some teens, scare tactics do make an impact. But we shouldn't tell someone not to do something simply because they might get pregnant or catch a disease. As teens have learned, there are ways around those consequences.

What we do need to teach them is the beauty of marriage and the wonder of God's design for his people. We need to teach

---

4   White, David. *Raising Sexually Healthy Kids* (New Growth Press/Harvest USA, 2014) p.11.

them that sex is a wonderful gift from God that reflects the love of Christ for us, his bride. His plan for us is good because he is good, and we glorify that goodness when we follow his plan for our lives. Ellen Dykas writes,

> We glorify God, and we experience the beauty and sanity of his design, when we follow his Word and thereby live in a way that reveals the wisdom of his character—a character the Bible reveals as worthy of worship and obedience. God's glory overflows in goodness to his creation. God is creator and loving Lord, so when we seek to glorify him with our bodies and through his ordained expression of our sexuality, the good gift of his design bears good fruit in our lives. This is his amazing grace revealed to us as we commit to express ourselves with the gracious guardrails of his created intent.[5]

We also need to talk openly with teens about the temptations that they face and discuss practical strategies for resisting such temptation. We live in a fallen world. Temptations are all around us. Television, movies and the internet only add to the temptations. It might mean helping our teens identify areas of weakness and helping them take drastic measures to reduce temptations. It always means keeping a line of conversation open.

But God has not left us to fight sin all on our own. He has graced us with his Spirit. We need to teach and remind our teens about what it means to have the Spirit of the living God within

---

5   Dykas, Ellen Mary. "Sexual Wholeness" in *Word-Filled Women's Ministry: Loving and Serving the Church*. Eds. Gloria Furman and Kathleen Nielson. Wheaton, IL: Crossway, 2015. p 180.

them, who reminds them of what is true and strengthens them to love and obey God.

Yet the reality is, teens are still sinners just like the rest of us. As Paul wrote, "For I do not understand my own actions. For I do not do what I want, but I do the very thing I hate" (Rom. 7:15). Some may violate God's commands in the area of sexual sin. There may be unplanned pregnancies. As parents, as members of Christ's church, if we find ourselves in such a situation with a teen, we need to be prepared for how we will help them through it.

We need to remember what Paul went on to write, "Wretched man that I am! Who will deliver me from this body of death? Thanks be to God through Jesus Christ our Lord!" (Rom. 7:24-25). The same grace that saves us from sin is the same grace that meets us in our sin. The grace of Christ is greater than our greatest sin. As 1 John 1:9 reminds us, "If we confess our sins, he is faithful and just to forgive us our sins and to cleanse us from all unrighteousness." Just as he met the woman at the well, Christ can meet a teen where she is and provide her the grace she needs through his gospel.

We all need God's grace to save us from our sins, to change and transform us into the likeness of Christ. God's grace can do that even in the midst of a teen pregnancy. His grace can use a pregnancy in a teen's life to show her how much she needs him. God's grace can use a teen's pregnancy to show her parents how much they need him. His grace can restore damaged relationships between parent and child. It can be an opportunity for a church to gather around and support a broken family. It can be a vehicle to show the world that God's grace brings life from the ashes of brokenness and despair.

CRISIS PREGNANCY COUNSELING

Though the teen has sinned and gone outside God's design for her, she now carries a new life. All of life is precious to God and each child is a blessing. When a teen learns she is pregnant, she is undoubtedly filled with fear, confusion, shame and help-lessness. In such an emotional state, the teen needs help and support from a place that values the life within her and can guide her through the difficult road ahead.

Practically speaking, one of the most important resources the church can utilize to help a teen and her family is the local crisis pregnancy center. There, the teen will find support, help, guidance and pregnancy counseling. She will be connected with other teen moms who understand what she is going through. She will be able to process with a counselor the difficult decision of whether she should raise the child herself or allow another family to adopt the baby. She will learn about the truths and horrors of abortion and about the joys of choosing life.

FOR THE FAMILY

The teen's family will need support from their church family. Something completely unexpected has happened that will change the course of their life forever. The parents may feel as though they have failed. They may feel shocked, shamed, angry, grieved or a combination of all the above. They may even be angry with God.

The family will undoubtedly need counseling. The parents will need a place where they can process their hurt, pain, sorrow, anger and broken trust. At some point, they will need to have counseling as a family, including the teen, where they can begin to find healing and restoration through God's grace.

If a church does not have a counseling center to provide counseling, it is important that church leaders know what resources for hurting families are in the area. The teen could also benefit from an older woman in the church who can take her under her wings, remind her of the gospel of grace, love her and walk with her through the challenges ahead.

God's design for sex is perfect and good, but we live in a fallen and broken world. We must prepare our children with the truth of God's plan for them and be ready and able to point them to the great grace of God that is theirs through Christ.

ON LIFE
AND THE
FAMILY

SEVEN

LOVING AND SERVING THROUGH THE REALITIES OF ADOPTION

BY KELLY ROSATI

My family's adoption story is a little different than most. My husband, John, and I never really struggled with the pain of infertility. Instead, we came face-to-face with two things: 1) the modern-day orphans in our own community who needed families and 2) the truth of God's call to believers in Christ to care for orphans. It was through these realities that God guided us through the adventure of adoption. We were living in Hawaii and actively involved in pro-life ministry, so it was natural that our thoughts would turn to advancing the *cause* of adoption. Little did we imagine the journey the Lord had *personally* in store for us.

After learning about the many children in foster care awaiting adoption right there on the islands, John and I spent much time discussing and praying about what God was calling us to do. Eventually, we decided that since we had a family and the kids needed one, we'd pursue adoption through foster care. We worked our way through reams of paperwork, hours of home study interviews, specialized training, background checks and physicals. Along the way, we learned about a baby boy whose foster mom was leaving the island for vacation and couldn't take him with her. He needed respite care, and we had an opportunity to provide it. We thought the practice would be helpful.

When I went to meet little Daniel, who was just under six months old, I didn't know what to expect. I did know, however, that Daniel's birth mother was a teenager who had used drugs and alcohol during her pregnancy. As a result, Daniel was born with symptoms of crystal methamphetamine and alcohol addiction. His foster mother told me that he would scream for hours on end.

During that first visit, though, he was lying quietly on the floor looking up at me. I asked to hold him, and as soon as he was in my arms he snuggled against my chest and fell asleep. It was love at first sight for me—I felt certain that I had just met my son. When John met Daniel, there was an instant bond between my husband and this gorgeous, needy little boy. It was beautiful to watch. We were completely smitten.

Eventually, we were able to adopt Daniel, and we became a "forever family." John and I were ecstatic even though parenting a baby with special needs was incredibly challenging. After adopting Daniel, we adopted three more children. Many might see our story and believe that the adoption of each of our four children was "the end," that happily-ever-after moment that we and our children had waited for. In truth, it was only the beginning.

THE TRUTH ABOUT ADOPTION

Adoption was the beginning of sleepless nights, attachment issues for little ones who had not been properly nurtured as babies, multiple visits to physicians and psychiatrists, learning disabilities, developmental delays and a great deal of wrestling on our part to forgive those who had caused such pain and trauma to our precious children. It was the beginning of learning—step by arduous step—about the lavish grace of God that is poured out when we commit to a lifetime of caring for little ones that are so immeasurably valuable to him.

In short, adoption—and particularly the adoption of children who have been abused or neglected—is never easy. But it is always worth it. It is a calling that is not a sprint to the finish line of signing the adoption papers, but a marathon of day-by-day, year-after-year parenting. And the Lord doesn't leave us to run that race alone, even though I've certainly felt that way at times!

We've had to learn that regardless of our feelings, God has been with us every step of the way. He has shown me the profound joy of motherhood. He has walked with me through tear-filled seasons when I wasn't sure how I would get from one end of each day to the other. And he has made it abundantly evident that his hand is upon my children in ways that could only be attributed to his divine power and guiding love.

A WORTHY INVESTMENT

As an orphan care advocate, I am passionate about articulating God's heart for children without parents and the church's responsibility to meet their needs. At the same time, we must be diligent to do all we can to prepare adoptive parents for the inevitable challenges that are unique to adoption.

Those who adopt "at-risk" children must be especially aware of the kinds of struggles they may face as they raise their children—and the church must do everything possible to come alongside adoptive families. Not every believer is necessarily called to adopt, but we *are* tasked with caring for orphans. In many cases, the best way we can do that is to offer love and support to the couples who have taken orphans into their hearts and homes.

There are many practical ways that congregations can surround the adoptive families in their midst. Respite care, meals, errands, housecleaning—the list goes on and on. It would be impossible to overstate the difference those seemingly small offerings can make in the lives of a family dealing with the turmoil and exhaustion that often accompany adopting kids from hard places.

The church and the culture at large should also be mindful that, while identifying suitable parents for hurting orphans is the necessary first step, a loving home doesn't automatically "fix" troubled and traumatized children—and it's not our job to "fix" them. What's more, the disciplinary measures and traditional parenting tools that would be effective for kids who are devloping normally are often the worst approach to take with children who have only known rejection, fear and neglect.

These kids have gone into survival mode—and what they most need from their adoptive parents is tireless patience, unconditional love, and a commitment to develop and nurture the parent-child relationship. As adopted children begin to realize that their new parents are on their side, they can let down their guard and trust can slowly build. Love can cast out the fear that drives their every move.

Recently John and I were approaching the end of a long and grueling season with one of our children, whose emotional outbursts and regular episodes of hours-long raging had left us all utterly depleted in every possible way. Here's how I described that situation in the book John and I co-authored, *Wait No More*:

> Even with the progress we've seen, there is no neat and tidy ending to the challenges we face with our daughter. No perfect, pretty bows. But there is God's grace and faithfulness in the midst of our messiness, failures, and brokenness. There is perseverance and hope in Christ. There is deep peace and even joy. There is amazing love . . .
>
> And there is this truth: We would never want to experience life without our daughter or any of our kids–whether that means life is easy or difficult. After all, where did we get the notion that the Christian life would be trouble-free? That's not what Christ promised us. But He did promise that He would be with us in the midst of everything. He has promised that in the end, we will overcome just as He has. He has promised that He loves each precious human being made in His image and likeness. And He calls His followers to reflect that same kind of love
>
> . . .
>
> Our children, like all children, are gifts from God.[1]

---

1   Kelly Rosati, John Rosati, *Wait No More* (Carol Stream: Tyndale, 2011), 164-165.

That is truly the beauty of adoption. Yes, caring for orphans is mandated in Scripture—and, yes, adoption is a beautiful picture of the gospel. However, for John and me and many other adoptive parents, our decision to adopt boils down to one simple truth: We love each of our children desperately, and we pour ourselves into them, day after day, because they are worth it. Their lives matter. That is the love that God has shown us, and it's the love *we* want to show as a result.

As I reflect on the path John and I have taken and consider this incredible family he had in the making long before adoption was even on our radar, I'm struck by one thing: Too often, adoption is seen as a "last-ditch effort" for infertile couples to have children. I want to see the church help recast a vision for adoption as God's "Plan A" for lonely and abandoned children in need of forever families. Adoption, after all, is close to the Lord's heart—we know that from verse after verse in Scripture that paints God as a "Father to the fatherless" and the one who "sets the lonely in families" (Psa. 68:5-6). He is passionate about seeing his people defend, protect and provide for orphans.

Thankfully, in recent years, the people of God have recommitted to this important mission. Many couples with birth children make the decision to adopt simply because they have love and a home to offer children who need both. And couples who are unable to conceive often discover that, despite the grief and disappointment that infertility causes, adoption truly was the Lord's best—and *first*—plan for them all along.

EIGHT

WANTED: PARENTS WILLING TO GET TOO ATTACHED

BY BRITTANY LIND

It has been almost one year since my husband and I brought our sweet baby boy home from the hospital. Memories of life before his arrival are faint. We can't imagine our day-to-day without his crinkled-nose smiles or excited shrieks of delight. Life with him is our new normal, and while being a mommy is more exhausting than I thought possible, it's also more joy-filled than I ever imagined.

This deep joy of motherhood, however, is mingled with sadness; the time is soon approaching when our days will no longer be filled with this little one's sweet shrieks of delight.

My heart aches knowing that while we have been able to enthusiastically cheer on his first attempts to crawl, it is unlikely we will be able to experience his first steps, first words or first day of school.

Our son is not terminally ill. This sweet baby we took home from the hospital nearly twelve months ago is our foster son. In the next month or two, he will likely leave our home and be adopted by his extended family members. We are grateful that our foster son has family members who want to raise him as their own. Still, deep grief fills our hearts knowing we may not be able to make this son we love a permanent part of our family. It is overwhelming to think of the day we will have to strap him in his car seat for the last time, kiss his big, soft cheeks and say our goodbyes.

At times, I'd wonder if we were crazy to get ourselves into this situation. Foster care is a messy, complicated process, filled with messy, complicated emotions. When we tell people he is our foster son, they usually commend us then quickly add, "I could never do foster care—I would get too attached."

But that's the point. We *are* "too attached".

WORTH THE RISK

My husband and I don't have any special ability to be foster parents. Our hearts are not unbreakable, and detachment is neither feasible, nor desirable. Attachment was our aim. Parents willing to get "too attached" are precisely what children in foster care need. And the need is enormous:

- There are more than 510,000 children in the foster care system in the United States, and of those kids, more than 100,000 are waiting to be adopted.[1] Nearly 19,000 will age out of the system every year before they have the chance to be adopted.[2]

- The kids who leave foster care without being linked to "forever families" are highly likely to experience homelessness, unemployment and incarceration as adults.[3] Thirty percent of homeless people in the United States were formerly in the foster care system.[4]

- The issue of attachment looms large. Having never learned how to attach to people or places, they struggle to find healthy relationships, stay in school and hold down a job later in life.[5]

Though our hearts will never be the same, by God's grace, we will survive the grief of giving up our foster son. The pain will be great but we have the coping skills and resources to deal with loss. If our foster son, on the other hand, were to go without the love and attachment he needs at this point in his development, he couldn't simply catch up later in life.[6] It is critical at each stage of development—infants, toddlers, young children—to learn how to attach.[7] What we've

---

1   "Foster Care Statistics." FosterClub. The Adoption and Foster Care Analysis and Reporting System, 2014. Accessed online, October 8, 2014. *https://www.fosterclub.com/article/foster-care-statistics*.

2   Tim and Wendy (last names not provided). Foster Parenting Podcast-Episode 50: "Forty Reasons We're Adopting Through Foster Care," *http://www.fosterpodcast.com/2008/11/05/episode-50-forty-reasons-were-adopting-through-foster-care/*

3   Ibid.

4   "The Hard Facts About Foster Care." Alameda County CASA. Court Appointed Special Advocates for Children, 2014. Accessed online, October 8, 2014. *http://www.casaofalamedacounty.org/District/1226-The-Hard-Facts-About-Foster-Care.html*.

5   Tim and Wendy, Foster Parenting Podcast, Episode 109: "All the Dirt on Foster Care and Why You Should Still Do It," *http://www.fosterpodcast.com/2011/10/26/episode-109-dirt-foster-care/*

6   Ibid.

7   Ibid.

learned is, even if children don't get to stay with the person they are attaching to, it's better for them to go through the pain of loss than to never attach to anyone at all. It is crucial therefore, for our son's sake that we risk the pain of getting "too attached".

Jesus says, "Whoever finds his life will lose it, and whoever loses his life for my sake will find it" (Matt. 10:39). We want to lose our lives for the sake of our foster son—not only because he needs us to, but because Christ met our even more desperate need. Every dirty diaper, every nighttime feeding, every heart-wrenching visit with his birth parents, and every court date and call from his social worker remind us that we are losing our lives. We are giving our hearts away to this little boy we have no promise of keeping. Still, no matter the sacrifices we make, they pale compared to all that Christ sacrificed to save us.

GIVER OF LIFE AND GOD OVER FOSTER CARE

Children are a gift. They are never ours to possess. That seems obvious with foster care but it is no less true with biological children. The Lord numbers the days we have with our children whether biological, adopted or fostered. We are never promised to keep any of the children entrusted to us. Whether I become a mother biologically or through foster care, my children belong to God, not me.

After suffering a miscarriage in the fall of 2013, we were delighted to find out we were expecting again four months later. A week after the positive pregnancy test, we received the phone call for our foster son. It has been a crazy season caring for the two children the Lord has given us within eight months, but I am beyond grateful and seek to remember daily that they are gifts given to me for as long as he sees best.

Contrary to what people may think (and have even expressed to us), the arrival of a new baby, a biological baby, doesn't make the loss of our foster son easier. We love our son and daughter with the same intensity—they are ours regardless of how they came into our home. The thrill of a new baby and the sorrow of anticipating the loss of the other don't cancel each other out. Deep joy and profound grief mingle together in our hearts.

In the midst of these muddled emotions, my husband and I have found much instruction and comfort in the book of Job. Though the giving and taking did not happen at the same time for Job, he blessed the Lord for both. He recognized that the same God who had given him everything was the same God taking it away and in all of his suffering, he "did not sin or charge God with wrong" (Job 1:22). He continued to acknowledge the goodness of God, both in the joyful blessings and in the painful takings. We, too, must join Job in blessing God for who he is and acknowledge that whether he gives or takes, he is a good God who can do all things and whose purposes cannot be thwarted (Job 42:2). He is not only the Creator and Sustainer of life but he is also God over the foster care system.

I don't claim to understand the "why" in his doings, and every fiber in my being would do anything to be my foster son's mommy forever, but the same God who gave and took our first child through miscarriage is the same God who brought our precious foster son to our home a few months later. The same God who gave us our precious daughter in the fall of 2014, is the same God directing the number of days our foster son will spend in our home. Daily, we are trusting that God is good in all of it. "He gives and he takes away, blessed be the name of the Lord" (Job 1:21).

Opening your heart and home to a foster child may seem risky but in reality, opening your heart to love *any* child is risky and requires a loss of self. But in losing ourselves, we gain. We grow in understanding how Jesus loved us and gave himself up for us. In seeking to love sacrificially, a picture of the gospel is painted for all to see. We pray many would see and put their faith in Christ. We pray too that our love, though imperfect, will lead our foster son to one day trust in Jesus, who gave him far more than we ever could. Lastly, our prayer and hope is that many would join us and risk becoming "too attached" for the sake of the children in need and the glory of the One who alone makes such risk possible.

NINE

HIGH RISK AND HIGH REWARD: LOVING THOSE WITH SPECIAL NEEDS

BY JENNIFER CASE CORTEZ

I remember the day we received the news.

The August heat radiated up from the pavement, but I shivered inside the psychologist's air-conditioned office. Fidgeting with my pen and notebook, I shifted positions on the sofa, trying to look, act and feel natural. My husband's professionalism and level-headed demeanor steadied me, as usual.

We settled into our seats, but my emotions wouldn't settle as easily. Anxiety, resolve, fear, curiosity and hope shoved and elbowed each other—all of them waiting to hear which one should step up and take the lead.

Finally, the child development expert joined us in her office. After welcoming us and setting the stage for her findings, she began delivering the results of the many tests she had administered to our son: the Woodcock-Johnson Tests of Cognitive Abilities, the Woodcock-Johnson Tests of Achievement, the IVA Continuous Performance Test, the Autism Diagnostic Observation Schedule, the Behavior Rating Inventory of Executive Functioning, the Behavioral Assessment System for Children, the Asperger's Syndrome Diagnostic Scale.

I remember smiling politely, nodding and trying to track along with one report after another. A virtual stranger who had spent only a few hours with our son was helping unlock a mystery about the child we'd cradled and nurtured for five-and-a-half years.

My husband and I looked at one another from time to time, affirming what we were hearing. We had been carrying around an ADHD diagnosis for a few weeks. Now we reached out to receive another box, this one full of the 2,000-pound words "Autism Spectrum Disorder."

On one hand, the diagnosis brought relief. It explained so much. The meltdowns in Walmart. The all-out declaration of war against the barber and his chair. The high-noon, Wild West showdowns between a tiny boy and his frazzled mother. This diagnosis meant our child's exhausting and puzzling behavior and defiance wasn't our fault—wasn't *my* fault. I laid some of my mother guilt down right there on the laminate flooring.

But what of the other hand? What would this mean for our family? For our son? For his future?

Four years later, you'll still find us on our knees crying out for help and asking God for these answers. Like manna from heaven, he faithfully gives us the grace and strength we need for each day—our own daily bread.

SUFFERING ISN'T A THROW-AWAY EXPERIENCE

My natural instincts drive me away from anything painful and difficult, but growing can be just that—painful. Parenting a child with extra challenges will open your eyes and heart in unexpected ways. You'll begin to see places where your child doesn't fit, where he or she stands out. You'll see dangers that don't exist for typical kids, snares that your son or daughter won't be able to avoid. The suffering you used to count as someone else's becomes your own, and the muscles of your heart begin to break down. Then you discover something surprising happening; your heart is stretching further and becoming stronger.

Doesn't pain often serve us in this way? As much as we seek to escape suffering, it has the power to deepen us in ways nothing else can, carving lines in our faces and sculpting our very souls, transforming us into something more beautiful than we were before.

People with disabilities, developmental delays, behavioral disorders and mental illness suffer. Those who love them suffer, too. As much as I shrink back from the word "disability" and search for positive descriptors and labels, the truth is, hardship is a very real part of the experience of anyone with special needs and challenges.

Some even argue that life is too cruel altogether for those with disabilities—that it would be more humane to remove them from the womb and spare them, their families and society the burden these disabilities bring. We must consider a person's potential "quality of life," we're told.

Margaret Sanger, birth control advocate and founder of the American Birth Control League, which later became Planned Parenthood, took the idea even further. A firm believer in eugenics and population control, Sanger said, "We want a world freer, happier, cleaner—we want a race of thoroughbreds. We want to make America the leading nation of the world physically, mentally, and spiritually."[1] Hailed as a hero by many for her work in reproductive rights, Sanger strongly supported the eradication of what she called "the unfit."[2] Though it seems Sanger earnestly sought to help women gain access to accurate information and to have a greater voice in their own lives, there was an undeniable dark underbelly to her work. In claiming to advocate for "a quality of life," Sanger also argued for death.

What Margaret Sanger failed to recognize was her own limited perspective, short-sightedness, biases and lack of understanding. She believed the human race would be better if only we could eliminate the genetic variants that make us vulnerable to weakness. How would we do this?

By eliminating the weak.

1   Lamb, W. Scott. "Margaret Sanger Wanted a Race of Thoroughbreds." *WashingtonTimes.com*. July 21, 2015. Accessed October 30, 2015. *http://www.washingtontimes.com/news/2015/jul/21/w-scott-lamb-margaret-sanger-wanted-a-race-of-thor/*.
2   Grossu, Arina. "Margaret Sanger, Racist Eugenicist Extraordinaire." *WashingtonTimes.com*. May 5, 2014. Accessed October 30, 2015. *http://www.washingtontimes.com/news/2014/may/5/grossu-margaret-sanger-eugenicist/*.

"ORCHID CHILDREN"— PART OF HUMANITY'S BEAUTIFUL DIVERSITY

Scientists are now finding that those very same genetic variations that determine the presence of disabilities also give rise to some of the most beautiful and remarkable children in the world, those who sometimes far surpass their typical peers. Known as "the orchid hypothesis," this fairly new way of thinking in genetics claims that while most of us are psychologically resilient like dandelions, the most vulnerable of us, when given the proper environment and care, can sometimes bloom spectacularly like orchids. "Together, the steady dandelions and the mercurial orchids offer an adaptive flexibility that neither can provide alone. Together, they open a path to otherwise unreachable individual and collective achievements. . . . This is a transformative, even startling view of human frailty and strength."[3]

Hans Asperger, a doctor who is credited with discovering what we now refer to as "the autism spectrum," worked with over 200 autistic children in Nazi-occupied Austria. He saw extraordinary potential in his own patients and fought valiantly to prevent them from being sent to extermination camps.[4]

Asperger's work to save his patients was certainly moral but also practical. He knew what everyone who loves someone with special challenges knows. Asperger understood that the same

---

3   Dobbs, David. "The Science of Success." *TheAtlantic.com*. December 1, 2009. Accessed October 30, 2015.
http://www.theatlantic.com/magazine/archive/2009/12/the-science-of-success/307761/.
4   "'Neurotribes' Examines the History—and Myths—of the Autism Spectrum." Hosted by Terry Gross. Fresh Air. *NPR*. September 2, 2015.
http://www.npr.org/sections/health-shots/2015/09/02/436742377/neurotribes-examines-the-history-and-myths-of-the-autism-spectrum.

bodies that house disability and dysfunction also hold bright and beautiful gifts, gifts that grow out of uniquely formed brains, gifts that might never be seen without drawing close or looking with a careful eye.

In the quest to extinguish weakness and suffering—then through eugenics, now through abortion—are we wiping out some of the most glorious and splendid diversity on the planet? Humanity is part of a delicate ecosystem. No human is intellectually or morally qualified to determine who gets to live and who doesn't. Like Sanger, we will always be limited by our own perspective and understanding.

A CALL TO EMBRACE AND NURTURE ALL HUMAN LIFE

What should we do then? How do we love beyond our natural abilities and limits? In our own strength we cannot. Loving well is a self-sacrificing and supernatural endeavor. This is why in a worldview without God, the pro-choice argument to "be realistic" when making the decision to remove a child with a difficult pre-natal diagnosis seems so plausible, humane even. Yet, who among us doesn't need to be accommodated and loved in spite of personal failures and frailties? Which one of us doesn't have special needs of one kind or another?

As Christians, we know that God has imbued every single human with dignity because every single one of us bears his image. We don't earn the right to be treated with respect because of our strength or our desirableness or how easy we are to care for. We have intrinsic worth because we're on this planet, because we're alive, because God breathed life into us.

As the mother of a twice-exceptional son, I can tell you that our family's life is riddled with difficulties. I have wept it out on the bathroom floor more times than I can count. There have been days when my own life has felt like a prison cell with claw marks lining all four walls. I can only imagine how difficult life must be for our precious son.

Yet isn't joy always tangled up with the difficulty of our daily lives? The human experience is marked with pain from birth until death, but it is also marked by joy and beauty and pleasure. We accept one with the other. Our son sees patterns in math that make my jaw drop open. He looks at the Florida State Seminoles mascot and asks, "Why does that Native American have bacon on his face?" He makes me burst into laughter at the oddest times because he sees the world in a delightfully odd way. He's a lot of things wrapped up in one body, as are we all.

OUTDO ONE ANOTHER IN SHOWING HONOR

We have a high and noble calling as Christians to bear one another's burdens and to fulfill the law of Christ (Gal. 6:2). We are designed to walk in relationship with one another and to raise one another up, to strengthen and love one another fiercely and well. We should be leading the charge of loving every life, discarding no one.

We have much costly and difficult work to do on many fronts to make the world a welcoming place for those who need extra care. Nothing calls us to sacrifice our comforts and our very selves more than love, but nothing in all the world is more precious. Nothing is more divine.

May God help and strengthen us.

WHAT CAN YOU DO?

In Your Thinking:

- Understand that every human life has intrinsic worth and dignity because all humans bear God's image.
- Recognize that our differences are a gift, not a curse. We are stronger together.
- Realize that God uses suffering for our good. Though suffering is caused by our rebellion against God, his great purpose for us will not be thwarted by our sin or its consequences.
- Make a clear distinction between fighting to end human suffering and fighting to eliminate humans who are suffering.

In Your Community:

- Draw near to those with special needs and disabilities with compassion and kindness; don't pull away from them in pity and fear.
- Learn more about the issues. Learn which elected officials support life and the rights of the disabled.
- Advocate for those with special needs with your voice and your vote.
- If you know a family or a person with special needs, ask how you might help them. Could they use a meal or a night out? Could they use help with the lawn or home maintenance? How can you support and encourage them?
- If you have the time, volunteer at your local school or local programs. Our local YMCA offers a wonderful program called Full Circle, for example.

In Your Church:

- Welcome every single child and family with special needs as a blessing from God, which they are!
- Prepare a list of community resources that you can give to families who have children with special needs. We need a lot of practical, everyday support.
- Partner with parents to develop a special education plan for their children at church, offering accommodations for each child.
- Enlist volunteers who can serve as a "special buddy" to each child who needs extra care during church hours.
- Consider starting a support group for families or caregivers. This is also an excellent way to reach out to your community with the good news of Christ's love for them.

On Your Knees:

- If you personally know a family who is caring for a child or adult with special needs, pray for them regularly.
- Put a photo of them on your refrigerator or bathroom mirror as a prayer reminder.
- Write out a prayer and mail it to them.
- Put their name on your calendar once a week to pray for them weekly.

"And the King will answer them, 'Truly, I say to you, as you did it to one of the least of these my brothers, you did it to me'" (Matt. 25:40).

DID YOU KNOW?

According to a 2010 U.S. Census report, approximately 56.7 million (18.7 percent) of the non-institutionalized, civilian population lives with a disability of some kind. Of children under the age of 15, about 5.2 million (8.4 percent) live with a disability.[5]

Two major studies reporting on the abortion rate of children with Down syndrome show that termination rates for those with a pre-natal diagnosis of Down syndrome are between 67-92 percent.[6]

ADDITIONAL RESOURCES

Joni and Friends International Disability Center, *http://www. joniandfriends.org/*.

Leading a Special Needs Ministry, Amy Fenton Lee, *https:// theinclusivechurch.com/*.

NeuroTribes: The Legacy of Autism and the Future of Neurodiversity, Steve Silberman

---

5   Brault, Matthew W. "Americans With Disabilities: 2010 Household Economic Studies." 2012. Web. 17 Dec. 2015. *http://www.census.gov/prod/2012pubs/p70-131.pdf*

6   Natoli, Jaime L., Ackerman, Deborah L., McDermott, Suzanne, Edwards, Janice G. "Prenatal Diagnosis of Down Syndrome: A Systematic Review of Termination Rates (1995–2011)" March 14, 2012. Web. 17 Dec. 2015. *http://onlinelibrary.wiley.com/doi/10.1002/pd.2910/full*.

TEN

LIFE IN THE BLENDED FAMILY

BY JOY ALLMOND

"Just make sure of two things: Under 40. And no kids."

This was what I said to the well-meaning people who thought I was getting too old to be single and wanted to play matchmaker for me. Not long after I made that statement, I found myself walking down the aisle toward a 44-year-old groom who happened to be the father of two sons.

Needless to say, I never imagined myself as a stepmom. The "no kids" criterion was not out of a disdain toward children. It's just that I always thought it would be a difficult role to step into.

As it turns out, I was right. Being a stepmom is the hardest thing I have ever done. But what I didn't expect was that this call to live beyond myself would reap blessings and growth.

CALLED TO LOVE

Becoming a stepmom stretched me in more ways than I imagined. Modern life is already complicated, and the plot thickens when stepfamily dynamics are thrown into the mix.

Where a blended family is concerned, simply making holiday plans and birthday celebrations can cause more-than-average stress; there are outside factors, like other biological parents and grandparents who have a say in the children's schedule.

More than that, the most difficult thing most stepmoms face is the lack of loyalty. My friend Laura Petherbridge, a blended family expert, explains: "She has all of the hard work associated with the mother role—helping with homework, cooking, carpooling, financial strain—but doesn't have the 'perks,' like love, loyalty and devotion that come along with being a biological mom."[1]

For this very reason, my role as a stepmom has been the most difficult, heart-wrenching part of my life. And the natural tendency is to be validated by other people for your work, your sacrifices and your love.

Yes, there are times I receive earthly satisfaction from my stepsons. I know they love me, and my husband is faithful in expressing his appreciation for my investment in their lives.

While this challenge brings heartache, I also see this as the single-most sanctifying aspect of my life. For those of us unfamiliar with this term, "sanctification" refers to the process of becoming more Christ-like.

Choosing to love and serve my stepsons—even though I don't know whether I will "earn" their loyalty—has helped me identify with

---

1   *http://billygraham.org/story/making-the-best-of-mothers-day/*

Christ in a unique way. The experience of learning to love someone else's child as my own is something I would never trade for a lifetime of comfort.

SPECIFIC CHALLENGES FOR THE CHILDREN

It goes without saying that the children of blended families face unique challenges and need special care. When there is a divorce (versus a death) in the background of the family's history, it is difficult to weekly adapt to two different households, with different rules and discipline styles.

If I had the power to fix one thing for my stepsons, it would be their church community experience. When a child is in a blended family, he or she is likely not around for each youth group event, summer camp experience, small group or Sunday school. This creates difficulty in establishing roots and deepening friendships within the church. Relationships require consistency, and children in blended families—by no choice of their own—do not bring this to the table.

At the time this chapter was written, the boys are 19 and 17. And sadly, they have no life-long relationships formed within the church. Thankfully, they have those friendships through the Christian school they attended, but as I look back on their childhood and earlier teen years, it occurs to me this could have been different had ministry leaders and other families with children their age been aware of the need to reach out to them, even in the "off weeks."

Just a little awareness—and effort—can make all the difference.

BLENDED FAMILIES AND THE CHURCH

All this said, the church need not be afraid of blended families. If you have not had experience with blended families within your church community, I promise you will, eventually. Here are some tips for engaging those families:

Acknowledge Our Roles

This can vary from church to church, but I have found that there are people who are afraid of saying "stepmom" or "step-dad." They just don't know what to do with us. But we live in a fallen world where people divorce and people die. Don't be afraid to use honest language, as long as it doesn't tear down or destroy.

Also, please understand that you may get a complicated answer when you ask, "How many kids do you have?" When I get that question, my answer is, "I have two stepsons." Most stepmoms don't have an answer that tidy, as many of them brought children of their own into the marriage. And some of those have had additional children with their current spouse.

In acknowledging their role, there must be understanding as you learn about the stepfamilies in your church. There are no simple answers, because—again—there is nothing simple about stepfamily dynamics.

Sympathize with Our Struggles

As you grow to understand the stepfamilies in your church, you can minister to them by sympathizing with their struggles.

Stepfamilies have unique challenges. One example of this is holidays. Holidays are often the most stressful times in the life of a stepfamily. For the biological parent, this is especially difficult because they are without their children, depending on the sharing arrangements. And if the blended family couple does not have other family in their lives, or nearby, these times can prove especially lonely.

By getting to know the stepfamilies in your church, you have a window into struggles like this one. And in doing so, the opportunity to minister presents itself. Perhaps there is a lonely blended family couple in your church without their kids at the holidays that could benefit from an invitation to your home this Thanksgiving or Christmas.

Include Us; Don't Single Us Out

Those of us who are in Christ, and who are also stepparents, possess spiritual gifts just like married couples in a traditional family.

The tendency is to segregate according to life stage. When it comes to church life, I have observed that stepparents get similar treatment as singles. Singles are often relegated to their own exclusive singles ministry, but they have so much to bring to the table when it comes to ministry and serving alongside married adults, children, seniors and students.

While there should be targeted ministry to stepfamilies within the church, we should not be singled out when it comes to serving. We are members of the Body of Christ, and we have a role to play.

Along the way, we will probably stumble upon someone else who is struggling through stepfamily life, and through our experiences, "we can comfort those in any trouble with the comfort we ourselves receive from God" (2 Cor. 1:4).

Most stepmoms don't grow up dreaming of marrying into a ready-made family. But this is a choice we make; not only a choice to marry a man with children, but a choice to love children who are not our own.

And these are often the hard choices—those which involve choosing life. Whether it's the unborn life, an elderly life, an orphan's life or a stepchild's life, the choosers of life make choices to love.

Yet even more so, the children of blended families need support, affirmation and love as they never made the choice to be in a blended family. Oh, to see the church step up and go the extra mile for these children!

ELEVEN

THE FAITHFULNESS OF GOD AND A SINGLE MOTHER

A TESTIMONY

BY SHANNON KOTYNSKI

As the youngest of three children, I grew up in a Christian home where I always felt the love and support of my parents. I loved Jesus as a young girl, but as I grew into the teen years, I started valuing the approval of others, the things of this world, and boys. I wanted to have fun, and the Christian faith was beginning to look and feel boring to me. Against my parents' wishes, I started dating guys who were not Christians. In my freshman year of college, I joined a sorority, went to parties regularly, and continued to date my high school boyfriend. During my second semester that year, life seemed to be going well, yet I found myself wrestling with conflicting desires.

One afternoon, I received a call from my mom while I was at school. She could tell something was wrong with me. She kept pressing, and I finally broke down and told her that I thought I was pregnant. After her urging, my friends and I went to a pharmacy to get a test. We took it back to my dorm, and about 10 of us crammed in to await the result. The result was positive, leaving us in total shock and horror. I was pregnant!

I cried and cried, along with my friends. I felt as if my whole world had come crashing down on me. The life had been sucked out of me. All of my dreams and hopes were shattered. At 18 and thoroughly enjoying sorority life, being a mom was the last thing I wanted to be. I knew right away, however, that this was the result of the life I had been living. Deep down, I also knew God was allowing this in my life to draw me back to him.

I nervously picked up the phone to tell my boyfriend the news. He was just as terrified as I was. I decided not to finish that semester of school and moved back home. I came back carrying shame, hopelessness and guilt. I didn't want to face all the people who thought I was a good Christian. I didn't want to step foot back into my church because I felt like such a liar and hypocrite. I had confessed my sin to the Lord, but now it was going to be exposed to everybody, and that was the most difficult part.

I'm so thankful for parents who welcomed me home with open arms. The first three nights after I moved back home, my mom slept in my little twin-sized bed with me while I cried myself to sleep. I will never forget the comfort she was to me. Despite fighting my parents about going back to church, they knew it was best for me and patiently took me anyway. I was overwhelmed by the love and generosity of my family and friends.

In the midst of all of this, I struggled with thoughts of depression and suicide. Thankfully, God remained faithful. He used my family and the church as an example of his love for me. I was reminded of how Jesus did not condemn the woman caught in adultery, but showed her love and mercy (John 8:1-30). Most of the people around me did not condemn me. They didn't tell me how wrong I was. They loved me and pointed me back to Jesus. John 3:17 says, "For God did not send his Son into the world to condemn the world, but in order that the world might be saved through him." Jesus took my condemnation upon himself on the cross so I could be forgiven. Yet it took years for that truth to sink in.

On October 2, 1999, my son was in my arms for the first time. How kind of the Lord to use a beautiful baby boy to bring me back to himself! It was the start of a new journey—one that came with many needs. God used the people around me to help fill those needs. My family threw a baby shower for us, and we were over-whelmed by the amount of gifts we received. We didn't have to buy one thing for our son for the first year of his life. I decided to go back to school and family members watched my son for free. A year later, I felt God leading me to get a part-time job and to put school on hold. I needed money to buy a car and other necessities. A doctor in our church offered me a job and let me pick my own schedule so that if I ever needed to bring my son, I could.

The greatest need I felt during this time was for a consistent father figure to be present in my son's life. His dad loved him so much and financially provided for him. There were times when he saw him every day for long stretches. But he was young and trying to figure things out as well. We ended up breaking up. He lived out of state at times, so his time with our son was inconsistent.

When he lived out of state, he would still come and see our son almost every weekend, though. During the week, my dad helped fill that role in a huge way, and I was always so incredibly grateful for any time a man would do something with him like teach him to throw a ball, take him fishing, take him to a sporting event, or most importantly, show him what a godly man looks like. I wanted him to be whole. It wasn't his fault that he was born to a teenage girl out of wedlock. I felt so guilty about that. I didn't want him to have to suffer the consequences of my sin, and I still have to continue to trust the Lord in that.

I'm so grateful that our God is a redeemer. He can take my mess and the mess handed down to my son, and make it beautiful for his glory. He gives us beauty for ashes (Isa. 61:3). Romans 8:28 has also been a beautiful promise to me, "And we know that for those who love God all things work together for good, for those who are called according to his purpose." He has done this in my life.

God not only used my pregnancy to wake me up spiritually, but he used it for my whole family as well. For the few years that preceded my pregnancy, both my sister and brother had been living a sinful lifestyle. They would both say that God used my circumstances to call all of us back to him. I've also seen the ways that this experience has impacted my son. Because his life hasn't always been easy, he has great compassion on others. I hear all the time from many people that he is a great kid and that there is something different about him; this is the work of the Lord. I can't wait to see how God is going to use him to bring glory to his name.

I'm so grateful for mentors in the church that poured into me and taught me how to follow Jesus. I learned to study God's Word as I joined different Bible studies. I was also given books, two of which were used mightily by God as turning points in my life, *Desiring God* by John Piper and *Surrender* by Nancy Leigh DeMoss.

God placed a group of godly friends in my life. I ended up marrying one of those friends six years after having my son. My son is now 16 years old and I am blessed to have three more awesome boys. I have come to experience the redemptive power of God! I never imagined I would have such an awesome godly husband and three more boys to love and care for.

Pregnant at 18, I thought my life had ended, but my life in Christ was truly beginning. God lovingly stopped me from being a strong-willed, rebellious girl and taught me that in surrender I find true freedom and joy. The Christian life is no longer boring to me. I now know the abundant life that Jesus died to give us, and nothing is more exciting than that!

TWELVE

REMEMBERING THE ELDERLY

BY KRISTIE ANYABWILE

In today's culture of idolizing youthfulness, casting off tradition and shunning authority, the value and beauty and honor of old age seems to have all but vanished. Elder care and retirement home construction is big business. The physical distance between parents and grand-parents seems as wide as the Gulf. Older people are literally being relegated to the back of the church, to neither be seen nor heard.

Church attendance was already thin when the senior choir sang on fourth Sundays. Now, there is no senior choir, only praise teams and worship bands. Bible studies often preclude older members because they either don't drive, or avoid driving in the evenings when these studies take place. Youth pastors, for example, focus on the needs of children and their families, but very few churches have ministries specifically charged with caring for the needs of senior members and their families.

Most would agree that caring for the soul is a primary responsibility of a pastor and that mutual care and concern is a primary responsibility of church members toward one another. In many of our church covenants, we agree to "exercise an affectionate care and watchfulness over each other." We promise to rejoice in each other's happiness and to bear one another's burdens and sorrows. How often, when we recite these covenantal promises, do we consider our senior saints? How might we exercise this care and what should we be watching out for in our older saints' lives?

Here are five ways the Scriptures demonstrate the Lord's blessings toward our senior saints and what we might learn from these blessings in order to be a blessing to them.

1. HONOR

Our primary responsibility toward our seniors is to honor them. Many of us are told from young childhood that we should honor our elders. We read in Leviticus 19:32, "You shall stand up before the gray head and honor the face of an old man, and you shall fear your God: I am the Lord." Commenting on this verse, Matthew Henry says,

> Those whom God has honored with the common blessing of long life, we ought to honor with the distinguishing expressions of civility; and those who in age are wise and good are worthy of double honor. More respect is owing to such old men than merely to rise up before them; their credit and comfort must be carefully consulted, their experience and observations improved, and their counsels asked and hearkened to.[1]

1   Henry, Matthew. *Matthew Henry's Complete Commentary on the Whole Bible.* The Bible Study App at Olive Tree, version 6.0. Retrieved from www.olivetree.com/bible-study-apps

What a way to honor our senior saints: consulting them for advice, improving upon their experiences so that we take the good and learn from their mistakes, and by listening to and accepting their counsel. Not only would we honor them through this, but we would be much better off ourselves.

In our previous church, my small group would sponsor senior luncheons, casual times of fellowship over a meal with our senior members. We would prepare home-cooked meals, provide a small gift to each of them such as a small potted plant, devotional book or ornament. Sometimes we had special musical selections by students or by our church choir. Mostly though, it was a time to honor our senior members and to share in fellowship with them. We sought to demonstrate our esteem of them, to let them know tangibly that we hadn't forgotten them. We identified senior members as those who were at least 60 years of age.

One year, we invited a man who was a few years shy of 60 and had a good laugh with him about his being too young to be at the "senior luncheon". His gray hair, leadership in the church and long-time service in the community had us fooled. None of us would ever have imagined that of all the folk present at the luncheon that year, he would be the one entering glory before our next gathering.

As I reflect back, what a sobering privilege it was to have honored this man, even before old age. We were reminded of Spurgeon's words, "Time is short, and it behooves each one to be working for his Lord, that when he is called home he may leave behind him something for the generations following." This man was not what we would call old, but he lived a very full and fruitful life. He worked hard, married well, raised two fine boys, devoted his life to Christ and the service of the church, dedicated much time to preserving the history and culture of his people and much more. His legacy of service placed him among the elders of the land and it was a gift from the Lord to have honored him along with our senior saints.

2. WISDOM

In Job 12, we read "wisdom is with the aged, and understanding in length of days. With God are wisdom and might; he has counsel and understanding" (Job 12:12-13). Interestingly, in these verses, we are told that with old age comes wisdom and understanding. There is something to be said about older saints who are viewing the breadth and depth of their life experiences through the lens of the gospel. They are seeing life through a larger lens.

Almost any decent photographer will tell you that the key to taking great photos is using the correct lens for the type of pictures you are taking. I read recently that photographers would rather shoot with a decent camera and a great lens rather than a great camera with a substandard lens. When choosing a lens, you must consider something called the focal length. The bigger this number, the greater focus on details. The lower the number is, the more you see but not in great detail.

When a believer is younger, they tend to focus on the big picture—there's a lower focal length for this person. Life is about "get all you can, can all you get, and sit on your can." We don't want to get bogged down with too many details. Older persons realize that real life is in the details—they bring a larger focal length with greater detail and clarity. The details of our identity in Christ cause us to zoom in on our lives and examine ways in which we live in light of our identity and ways in which we have broadened our view so as to blur our ability to see clearly where we might need to apply better wisdom to our life situations.

Older saints see that decision you're making now and can zoom in to point out flaws in your process, holes in your thinking, stumbling blocks you had not considered because you want to get that promotion or man at any cost. You want to take shortcuts now that will cost your family in the future.

How many times have I heard my grandma say, "I wouldn't do that if I were you"? I'd respond in that youthful, exasperated tone "Why not?" She'd then proceed to tell me about all the potential pitfalls that could result from my actions. Of course, I didn't believe her and didn't think she knew what she was talking about. But sure enough, she was right. Washing a red shirt with white laundry will turn the entire load pink. Running from a dog will get you chased and bitten. The wisdom of the aged is wisdom indeed, and we would be wise ourselves if we learned to heed their wisdom and counsel.

3. HOPE

Of all people, our elderly should be the most hopeful of all.

> Do not cast me off in the time of old age; forsake me not when my strength is spent. . . . But I will hope continually and will praise you yet more and more. My mouth will tell of your righteous acts, of your deeds of salvation all the day, for their number is past my knowledge. With the mighty deeds of the Lord GOD I will come; I will remind them of your righteousness, yours alone. O God, from my youth you have taught me, and I still proclaim your wondrous deeds. So even to old age and gray hairs, O God, do not forsake me, until I proclaim your might to another generation, your power to all those to come (Psa. 71:9, 14-18).

David confidently prays that the Lord would preserve him in his old age. He recognizes that his physical strength is waning and that he will need strength outside of himself to continue running his race with perseverance. His confident hope in the Lord ushers forth unending praise and testimony of God's goodness and faithfulness in keeping him. Where does this hope come from? He remembers the past faithfulness of the Lord from his childhood, which fuels his trust in God for his future. Until his dying day, he will proclaim the goodness of the Lord, giving hope to the generations to come.

Hope from ages past engenders hope for the future. In the church especially, we should look to those who have been through times of testing, trial and temptation and have come through those times hopeful in the Lord and recipients of his faithfulness. We should follow their example but remember that we do not finally look to elder saints or anyone else for identity and hope and wisdom. We look to Christ alone, knowing our hope is found in him.

4. FRUIT

I lived on a tropical island for many years, and my favorite time of year was mango season. Mangoes are fairly easy to grow, but they don't produce much fruit the first couple of years you plant them. However, the older the tree, the deeper its roots run, making it more established in the soil and environment in which it was planted. These mature trees are the ones that bear much fruit.

Similarly, the Bible teaches us that old age is no barrier of fruit. In fact, the latter years may be the most fruitful years. "The righteous flourish like the palm tree and grow like a cedar in Lebanon. They are planted in the house of the LORD; they flourish in the courts of our God. They still bear fruit in old age; they are ever full of sap and green, to declare that the LORD is upright; he is my rock, and there is no unrighteousness in him" (Psa. 92:12-15).

Those whose lives have been marked by righteousness and holiness continue to bear fruit as those early seeds of faith have taken deep root through prayer, grown into tiny plants through time in God's Word, blossomed through fellowship with the saints, and grown sturdy through discipling relationships. We see this in the life of the prophetess Anna, whose husband died after seven years of marriage, leaving her widowed into her 80s. She stayed in the temple, worshiping, fasting and praying night and day (Luke 2:36-38). Her life remained fruitful well into her elder years. May we give God praise for faithful, fruitful elder saints in our churches.

5. REST

We first meet Joshua, who Moses charged with raising up an army to fight and defeat the Amalekites, as a young man (Exod. 17:8-14). Joshua becomes an assistant to Moses, going with him up Mount Sinai to receive the Ten Commandments (Exod. 24:13). He alerts Moses to the raucous Israelites as they worshiped the golden calf (Exod. 32:17); spies the land of Canaan and, along with Caleb, brings back a favorable report of the land (Num. 14:6). Only Joshua and Caleb lived of the first generation of Israelites (Num. 14:38). And he's the successor to Moses as leader of the people of Israel (Num. 27:12-22). When Joshua steps into Moses' role, he leads the Israelites across the Jordan into the Promised Land (Josh. 3:1-17). He's at the helm as God miraculously helps his people defeat Jericho (Josh. 6:1-27). Joshua leads them in conquering their enemies to take possession of the land God had promised them. He was a busy man!

About half way through the book of Joshua, we learn that Joshua was "old and advanced in years"(Josh. 13:1), yet the Lord had much left for him to accomplish. He finished distributing land to the tribes of Judah that Moses had assigned years before. And once all the land had been distributed, the Lord gave Joshua land that he had requested for himself, "Timnath-serah in the hill country of Ephraim. And he rebuilt the city and settled in it" (Josh. 19:50). Joshua lived a long time after that and was able to enjoy the rest that the Lord had given Israel from their enemies. In his final days, Joshua poured out his heart for the people, reminding them of all the Lord had done for them and promised to them. He encouraged, warned and instructed them before his death at 110 years old (Josh. 23-24).

Although Joshua and the people of Israel experienced a season of peace, Joshua did not fritter that time away in worthless pursuits. He worked until the end. The rest he pursued was not a long hiatus from work and from serving others—it was finishing the work that the Lord had for him. It was using his old age to exhort, remind, encourage, warn and instruct the young folk in the words and ways of the Lord. He may have rested from hard, manual labor, but he worked hard to impart the wisdom and knowledge that God had given him over his many years of serving the Lord.

We encourage rest in our senior saints by taking in their wisdom and passing it on to the next generation, just as they so often model for us. "He established a testimony in Jacob and appointed a law in Israel, which he commanded our fathers to teach to their children, that the next generation might know them, the children yet unborn, and arise and tell them to their children, so that they should set their hope in God and not forget the works of God, but keep his commandments" (Psa. 78:5-7).

Honor. Wisdom. Hope. Fruit. Rest. These blessings are just a sampling of the ways the Lord has demonstrated his kindness to our senior saints. We would do well to honor our senior saints, to glean from their wisdom, to model their hopefulness, to join them in fruitful ministry, and to rest in our old age from manual labor, but not from serving the Lord and passing on the legacy of faith to future generations.

LEARN TO LISTEN, AND LISTEN TO LEARN

Of course, what this requires of us is that we spend time with our senior saints. It is often in the stories our older friends tell that we see the Lord's blessings practically applied to their lives. Listen to their stories of love, loss and life. We should patiently and intently listen to the stories that they tell. These stories are not just reminders of the past, but they are history as seen through one person's eyes. They serve as encouragements and warnings to us that we might not repeat their mistakes but that we might learn from them and walk in wisdom.

As you listen to the many stories of our older saints, be attentive to what these stories teach about perseverance, faith, prayer, maturity, rejoicing in hope, patience in tribulation, power of prayer, different perspectives on culture and society, defying odds, humility, gratitude, and so much more. There is wisdom to learn if we just slow down and listen. We should be eager to learn to listen to our senior saints and listen in order to learn valuable life lessons from them. They have a full range of life experiences that they are now placing under the banner of the gospel.

EQUIPPING THE BODY TO SERVE THE ELDERLY

Pastor Brian Croft offers five key insights in his book, *Caring for Widows*, which are focused on the widow, but I believe can also be applied to how we care for the elderly. He directs these suggestions to pastors, but they are helpful for us all to keep in mind as we serve our older saints. His suggestions are paraphrased and summarized here:

1. Pastors should preach with special application for how we might love and care for our elderly, and lay-people should seek to apply these suggestions. We can all teach about caring for the elderly in small groups, classes or even in relationships with one another.
2. Pray for the elderly in public gatherings. Pray for specific health or personal concerns, gospel opportunity and fruit, hope in God to flourish, and connection to the body of Christ.
3. Provide details to inform the body of Christ about who the elderly are and opportunities to serve them.
4. Pastors must practice what they preach. Teachers must be consistent with their instruction. Leading by example is essential.
5. Praise members, friends and fellow believers for specific ways they care for our elderly.[2]

---

2   Brian Croft and Austin Walker, *Caring for Widows: Ministering God's Grace* (Wheaton, IL: Crossway, 2015). Kindle version, p. 91-95.

Why should Christians care for those often invisible, elderly members of our churches? Because love compels us. We love our seniors because Christ loved them first and best. Our love for our older saints is a dim reflection of the love Christ has for them, but we are still called and compelled to love one another just as Christ has loved us (John 13:34).

Sometimes it's hard to love someone we seem to have little in common with. Ed Welch says it so well, "We move toward others in love. Because we are relentlessly pursued, especially when we are not worthy of such pursuit, we also become pursuers. We turn toward others and move in their direction. That is how the kingdom of heaven works. Sin scatters people; grace draws us toward each other."[3] We can only be drawn to others by the grace and Spirit of God. By his grace, we are able to move toward one another in love, sharing in all that we have in common in Christ, and rejoicing in the differences that make our fellowship all the sweeter.

TO THE ELDERLY SAINTS

What a treasure you are to us! The Lord has given you a lifetime of experiences wherein you have learned to trust him. You have seen the Lord show up time and time again in your need. You have seen his promises come to pass — his promise to never leave or forsake you, to answer your cries, to provide, to guide, to strengthen, to comfort, to restore, to give courage, protect, to discipline you for your good, to help you persevere, to grow you in holiness, to give you a peace that passes understanding, to satisfy, to make you

---

3   Welch, Ed. "Moving Toward People". CCEF Blog. Posted May 6, 2010. *www. ccef.org/resources/blog/moving-toward-people*

fruitful. You have stood on the promises of God's Word and have found him faithful. Thank you for your faithful witness. May he keep you in his grace, and may we better love and serve and listen to you that we might together grow up into maturity in Christ until he takes us home.

THIRTEEN

THE WIDOW AND THE CALL OF THE CHRISTIAN

BY KRISTIE ANYABWILE

They had a loving, normal, peaks-and-valleys kind of marriage. They raised four children to adulthood. He ran a small carpentry business, and she worked as a nurse. One day, his life became a battle against sickness. She had prayed for him for years and trusted the Lord to do his work in her husband's life in his way and his time. When the news of his cancer came, so did an eternal perspective. A wife's praying years produced that seed, which would sprout into gospel conversations and flower into saving faith for a dying husband. You see, as he was losing his physical life to cancer, he gained spiritual life in Christ.

When his strength was present, they read the Scriptures, prayed and sang hymns together. He attended church as regularly as he could and enjoyed the sweet fellowship of the saints. Their joy was full in the midst of their trial as she witnessed his inner man being renewed day-by-day. The Lord used her husband's suffering to bring him to the saving knowledge of Christ. Now he knew that he could not meet God on his own terms. So, he repented of his life of sin and trusted in Christ for forgiveness and reconciliation with God.

Though hard, she wouldn't trade their trial for anything. He spent his final breath in the loving arms of a faithful wife, who prayed him into the arms of Another. One whom she had trusted from the time of her youth. One whom she knew would never leave nor forsake them. One who called her to be a widow.

But what now for this grieving widow? How should the church love and care for her? How should she think about life and ministry when so much of her life and ministry rightly revolved around caring for her husband, children and home?

Pastor Brian Croft, in his book, *Caring for Widows: Ministering God's Grace*, calls attention to the neglect of widows that seems prevalent in the church today. He says,

> For some reason, a large portion of the evangelical church has missed the biblical warrant to care for widows, while still engaging in care for the fatherless and the poor. Even those who see widows as being among those whom God particularly calls his people to protect, provide for, and nurture still sometimes fail to make it a priority. In part, this neglect could stem from an inability to know how best to care for a widow. As a

result, widows still remain largely overlooked and forgotten in the church.[1]

But this has not always been so. God highly honors and cares for widows. He issues hard consequences on those who mistreat or devalue them. In fact, the Bible is full of wonderful stories that illustrate the Lord's heart toward widows and how we should follow his example as we see and serve the widows among us.

SPECIAL HONOR

Widows are not cranky, old, bitter women who line the back pews and serve as professional weepers for funerals. They are made up of the young and old, rich and poor, moms and barren. These women are beautiful, honored and loved by the Lord. Yes, they may be lonely at times, but they are not without hope, as their hope is set fully on God in prayers and supplications for themselves and others (1 Tim. 5:5).

From the early pages of Scripture, we understand that God is serious about our treatment of widows. He says, "You shall not mistreat any widow or fatherless child. If you do mistreat them, and they cry out to me, I will surely hear their cry, and my wrath will burn, and I will kill you with the sword, and your wives shall become widows and your children fatherless" (Exod. 22:22-24). The Lord commands us not to harm widows, but to show them special favor in our treatment of them.

In biblical times, wives would have been cared for and protected by God through their husbands and children. When a woman's

---

1   Brian Croft and Austin Walker, *Caring for Widows: Ministering God's Grace* (Wheaton, IL: Crossway, 2015). Kindle version, p. 14.

husband died, and she had no means of support through family, the Lord himself would hear their cry and come to their rescue. "He executes justice for the fatherless and the widow, and loves the sojourner, giving him food and clothing" (Deut. 10:18).

The Lord also promised special honor and blessings upon those who showed generosity toward widows. "At the end of every three years you shall bring out all the tithe of your produce in the same year and lay it up within your towns. And the Levite, because he has no portion or inheritance with you, and the sojourner, the fatherless, and the widow, who are within your towns, shall come and eat and be filled, *that the Lord your God may bless you in all the work of your hands that you do*" (Deut. 14:28-29, emphasis added). We should be generous toward the widow, using our abundance to meet her need.

Our lavish generosity to others because of the Lord's lavish generosity toward us is cause for rejoicing. The Lord calls us to rejoice in serving and giving to the widow. "And you shall rejoice before the Lord your God, you and your son and your daughter, your male servant and your female servant, the Levite who is within your towns, the sojourner, the fatherless, and the widow who are among you, at the place that the Lord your God will choose, to make his name dwell there" (Deut. 16:11, 14). In response to the freewill offerings made during the Feast of Weeks, the people rejoice. The worshipers rejoice in serving and giving. The widow rejoices in receiving. Shouldn't this be so in the body of Christ today as well?

In the New Testament, Paul instructs Timothy to encourage the church to honor widows. Specifically, the church is to honor a widow's character, her family and her service. These instructions demonstrate both a pastoral and practical concern and care for widows in the body of Christ. Even before a woman becomes a widow, her pastor would be shepherding her throughout her marriage, watching over her life as she cares for her husband, children and those in need so that her reputation and the reputation of Christ is upheld.

In widowhood, her pastor must encourage her to conduct herself in a manner that is beyond reproach (1 Tim. 5:7), to continue bearing fruit through her good works (1 Tim. 5:10), to avoid loafing about (1 Tim. 5:13), so that Satan would have no occasion for slander (1 Tim. 5:14). The church is not to usurp or override the role of family to care for their widowed mother or grandmother but is to encourage them to take responsibility for her care. There even seems to be an implied disciplinary response from the church for families who neglect to care for the widow (1 Tim. 5:7-8), for surely one who has denied the faith and become worse than an unbeliever would be subject to disciplinary action by the church. The widow's pastor would emphasize the priority of family to provide for her before the church would step in to care for her physical needs (1 Tim. 5:7-8, 16).

SPECIAL CARE

Throughout the Bible, we are given pictures of young widows like Ruth and Abigail, older widows such as Naomi and Anna, the destitute widow of Zarephath, the poor widow who gave out of her poverty, the persistent widow who begged for justice and others. What you see in the lives of each of these women as you survey their stories is the Lord's commitment to watch over and to provide for them.

God's people are instructed in how they should regard the widow. They must not be mistreated (Exod. 22:22-24); they should be provided for (Deut. 14:28-29); we should be generous toward them (Deut. 24:19-22); we should show them kindness, mercy and righteous judgment (Zech. 7:8-10).

Three widows are pictured in the book of Ruth, and in this account God's heart, provision and protection is made clear. As the story unfolds, Naomi is concerned with the practicalities of having three widowed women traveling with meager means to a land that is foreign to them all (Ruth 1:6-7). Despite her pleading for the younger widows to stay in Moab and return to their mother's homes and remarry, Ruth decides to remain with Naomi (Ruth 1:8-14), even when her sister-in-law, Orpah, agrees to turn back home. Although Judah was her hometown, Naomi had been living in Moab for some time, so her return to Judah would come as a great surprise to her family and friends living there. Ruth is resolutely determined to follow her mother-in-law in faith, trusting in Naomi's God to be with them as they go (Ruth 1:16-18).

Ruth is a young woman eager for the spiritual and practical guidance of an older woman, who happens to be her widowed mother-in-law. Ruth attempts to meet their practical needs as she is the younger more able-bodied of the two (Ruth 2:2). Naomi provides wisdom that Ruth, in her youth and unfamiliarity with the law and tradition, had not considered. She encourages Ruth to work in the field of her late husband's relative, Boaz. Naomi then instructs Ruth in properly introducing the prospect of marriage to Boaz as her kinsman-redeemer who would give her rest from the weary life of widowhood and take care, not only of herself, but her mother-in-law as well (Ruth 3:1-13, 4:1-12). In caring and providing for these widows, the Lord was also caring and providing for future generations. Ruth does indeed marry Boaz and the story of these two widows culminates in not just a marriage, but a lineage and heritage from which the King of Glory would descend (Ruth 4:18-22).

God's special care of widows is also seen in the life of Abigail. As the wife of foolish Nabal, Abigail covered her husband's foolishness with wisdom, grace and generosity. After her husband died, she was a widow a short time before David took her as his wife. Surely his attraction to her stemmed from her humility and discernment in responding David's request for provisions (1 Sam. 25:1-42). Then there is the destitute widow of Zarephath whom the Lord provided for as she sacrificially gave her last morsels to Elijah, trusting that the same Lord who was using her to provide for Elijah in his time of need would provide for her as well (1 Kings 17). What confidence. What faith. What hope in things unseen!

Even in the New Testament, we see God's provision as we learn of the unrighteous judge who did right by a widow because of her persistence (Luke 18:1-5); of the disciples who recognized that certain widows were not being served in the church, and how the Lord provided deacons to serve them (Acts 6:1-5); of the servant Dorcas whom the Lord used to provide tunics and other garments to the widows in Joppa. Over and over, we see the Lord's heart toward widows and orphans and the poor.

How much more should we, as the body of Christ, take special care of the widows in our churches? The Lord watches over and upholds widows (Psa. 146:9). And he summarizes true religion as being seen in two ways: caring for the souls of others by visiting and showing special concern for widows, and caring for our own souls by keeping ourselves unstained from the world (Jam. 1:27). As a church, we can and must do better in demonstrating special honor and care of our widows.

SERVING OUR WIDOWS

How might Christians better serve the widows in our churches? It may be uncomfortable to enter the life of a grieving woman, but we must. Grieve with her, as we are called to mourn with those who mourn. Share Scripture with her. Express sympathy and provide words of encouragement. Send her a card or personal note. Sit with her and listen to her stories. Greet her at church and invite her to sit with your family in worship service. Involve her in your Bible study or small group. Pray with her. Invite her to outings and holidays with your family. Serve her in practical ways, such as mowing her lawn, light home maintenance, taking her out for the day to a garden or show. There are many practical ways we can be involved in their lives.

TO THE WIDOW

We watch you in the back pews and somehow you have become invisible to us. As we have recalled the lives of many women in Scripture, we not only see the Lord's material provision, we see his loving compassion and tender mercy for each of these godly women. Naomi's joy returns. Ruth grows in wisdom. Abigail's discernment keeps her people safe. The widow of Zarephath sees the Lord's faithfulness. The persistent widow perseveres. Dorcas' life is restored. May the Lord help us to remember how he has used widows to teach us about his care for you, precious sister—his provision and sacrificial love, the power of prayer, perseverance and so much more! May he help us to be mindful of you and to imitate his care in the way we serve you.

ON PROTECTING LIFE

FOURTEEN

BECOMING A PRO-LIFE FIRST RESPONDER IN YOUR COMMUNITY

BY CYNTHIA HOPKINS

I recently heard the prayer request of a friend from my Sunday School class who signed up for volunteer training at our local pregnancy center. Feeling unsure, Catherine asked for prayer because she didn't think she was equipped to effectively serve women and men facing difficult pregnancy decisions. "I know God is calling me, but I don't know anything about the issue, and I am petrified," she candidly lamented. While I wanted to encourage her in her decision to serve, I also wanted to laugh out loud. You see, Catherine could have been me many years ago when I decided to volunteer at my local center. Fear and apprehension reigned supreme.

Twenty-five years and countless prayers for wisdom later, I am still actively helping people choose life and humbled to be serving God in such an important work. He has equipped and sustained me along the way. Today, I am dedicated to helping others realize their influence in the battle against abortion. With more than one million abortions performed in the United States every year, there is much work still to be done.[1]

As Christians more fully realize the "life and death" nature of an abortion decision, I pray women in the church will, like Catherine, put aside fears, step out in faith, and trust God as he equips them to serve. Perhaps you are someone who cares deeply for the unborn, or maybe you have an abortion in your past and now want to help other women. Or, maybe you are like me and have seen firsthand the devastation abortion can bring mothers, fathers and families. No matter your motivation, if God is calling, there is a place for you to use your gifts to protect and nurture life.

There is urgent need for people who can be "first responders" when women are considering abortion. The term first responder is often used to describe someone trained to attend to an emergency or crisis. A paramedic at the scene of an accident is an example. As the actions of a paramedic can affect the outcome of a medical emergency, the words and deeds of someone responding to a pregnancy crisis can alter the trajectory of a pregnancy decision. Within our pro-choice culture, there cannot be too many pro-life first responders.

There are two prominent ways you can serve as a pro-life first responder and make a difference in the life of a person making a

---

1   Jones RK and Jerman J, Abortion Incidence and Service Availability in the United States, 2011, Perspectives on Sexual and Reproductive Health, 2014, 46(1):3-14. Retrieved from *www.guttmacher.org/pubs/journals/psrh.46e0414.pdf*

pregnancy decision. Volunteering or working at a pregnancy center is a meaningful and rewarding experience, but even if there is no center close to you, keep in mind that anyone with a calling to be involved can be a pro-life first responder in the communities where they live, work or serve, including the church.

FIRST RESPONDERS AT THE PREGNANCY CENTER

Pregnancy center ministry is where many people begin their pro-life service. These faith-based, non-profit organizations[2] exist to offer compassion, hope and help to women (and men) facing difficult pregnancy decisions. The 1973 Supreme Court decision permitting abortion-on-demand in all 50 states shocked many believers. Realizing the need for pro-life first responders, Christians started pregnancy centers in their communities to offer life-affirming alternatives to women and couples who might feel abortion is their only realistic option. Compassionate care, free pregnancy tests, ultrasounds, abortion information, parenting classes and material assistance are just some of the services these centers offer.

Serving as a first responder in a pregnancy center can be intimidating initially, but training is available. Women who allow God to equip them, while relying on the guidance of the Holy Spirit, often experience immense joy in being part of a changed heart and a saved life. Furthermore, pregnancy center first responders get to share the Good News of salvation in Jesus Christ with those they serve. Imagine the angels in heaven

---

2   Also called Crisis Pregnancy Centers, Pregnancy Resource Centers, and Pregnancy Care Centers

rejoicing when an abortion vulnerable woman chooses eternal life. She is now empowered to choose life for her unborn baby and abundant life for her family!

While being a first responder in a local pregnancy center is an amazing privilege, it can also have difficult moments. Women can experience discouragement while serving. I remember the first time I learned that a client I had poured into made the decision to abort her baby. It is heartbreaking and can lead to disappointment, discouragement and doubt. In both joy and disappointment, it is important to draw near to our great God, finding the strength we need to care for others in the love he has for us.

Only as we find our satisfaction in Christ can we guard against "compassion fatigue." Our responsibility is to offer compassion, hope, and help to those considering abortion, according to our training, and to follow the Spirit's guidance. Ultimately, the pregnancy decision is the responsibility of the woman we are serving. We are called to obey; it is God who changes hearts.

The exciting news is that each year, eight out of 10 women who visit a Care Net-affiliated pregnancy center with thoughts of abortion subsequently choose to carry their babies to term. Since 2008, that's more than 460,000 decisions for life because of the dedication of pregnancy center staff and volunteers.

FIRST RESPONDERS IN THE CHURCH

While women who are called to work at their local pregnancy centers minister in amazing ways, pro-life first responders are also needed within our churches. Sadly, many women who have abortions in the U.S. every year attend churches. According to a recent LifeWay Research study commissioned by Care Net, four out of

10 women who chose abortion did so during a time when they are actively attending a Christian church.[3]

While this news is staggering, we should not be discouraged. There is hope to turn this trend around. Equipped with an understanding of the issue and a willingness to act, women in the church can become an integral part of changing the landscape of abortion within their own congregations. It can be as simple as educating yourself on the issue of life and being available to someone considering abortion.

Consider this example of a woman in the church helping another woman with her pregnancy decision:

> After Allison discovered that she was pregnant, she found the courage to talk to Bethany, a friend from her Wednesday night Bible study. Allison knew Bethany had experienced a teen pregnancy years earlier and thought maybe she could help her. Bethany listened attentively as Allison shared her circumstances, concerns and intention to find an abortion.
>
> Bethany hugged Allison and thanked her for trusting her with this news. She asked questions and learned that Allison was frightened about how her parents would react to her pregnancy since they were leaders in the church. Bethany told Allison that it is normal to not want to disappoint your parents and that many women think abortion will erase their problem. She told Allison that she, too, had thought that at one time.
>
> Bethany continued to ask thought-provoking questions and

---

3   McConnell, S. (2015). Study of Women Who Have Had an Abortion and Their Views on Church. Nashville, TN: LifeWay Research.

explored what Allison knew about God's perspective on abortion and life. She made sure Allison understood what the Bible says about unborn life. She also shared some of the things she learned when she was pregnant with her first child, including the fact that an unborn baby has a beating heart as early as 22 days after conception.

Lastly, Bethany offered to help Allison get a free ultrasound from their local pregnancy center so she could truly have all the information she would need to make her decision. While having a child was not in Allison's plans, she began to see how her plans could change to include welcoming her baby. She abandoned her decision to abort and accepted support from Bethany, her church, her parents and her new friends at the pregnancy center.

This scenario provides a glimpse into the work of a life-affirming first responder in the church. We can see how Bethany made a positive impact in the woman's pregnancy decision. It's important to point out that women like Allison often make their pregnancy decisions in isolation. Many go to an abortion clinic without the information needed to fully understand their choice.

We can learn from Bethany's approach—helping a woman facing a pregnancy decision does not have to be complicated. It simply means sharing truth with compassion while being thoughtful about questions and responses. It also involves keeping the hurting woman's needs at the forefront of the conversation. Not every woman will choose life as Allison did, and pregnancy centers are not in every community, but there are a few principles that any woman of faith can apply in such a life-altering conversation.

THREE GUIDELINES FOR FIRST RESPONDERS

1. Listen well and often. Listening is the cornerstone of connection with anyone in crisis. Listening well means you are trying to understand the other person and her perspective. If you don't listen well, you might miss the underlying issues causing a woman to consider abortion. Listening well also provides you the opportunity to reflect back what you have heard and to gently challenge any inconsistencies in the woman's reasoning about her decision.

2. Normalize feelings. As foreign as some feelings and emotions might seem to you, they are real and valid to the woman in crisis. Normalizing these feelings doesn't mean you agree with them, but it does let her know she is not alone in her feelings. There are many women whose first reaction to pregnancy is abortion. Don't worry that saying, "It's normal to think about abortion," sends the message that "abortion is ok." Instead, it tells her: "Your feelings are important." Validating her feelings shows respect and keeps the door open for further conversation.

3. Engage from a place of compassion *and* truth. While truth is foundational to any conversation you have with a woman considering abortion, truth alone is not always compelling to a person in dire circumstances. Throughout his public ministry, Jesus met the needs of hurting people, including their spiritual, physical, emotional and relational needs. His uncompromising focus on the Father's truth, charged with compassion and love, transformed countless lives during his time on earth. Consider the woman caught in adultery in the gospel of John. Jesus did not back down from the truth about her sin. He presented her a compassionate alternative with no condemnation when he told her, "Go and sin no more" (John 8:9-11). We must do the same as we share biblical truth compassionately with women who are hurting so much they are willing to consider abortion. The Apostle Paul helps us remember that love and truth go hand and hand. "If I speak in the tongues of men and of angels, but have not love, I am a noisy gong or a clanging cymbal" (1 Cor.13:1).

Just as training is available to women who choose to serve in pregnancy center ministries, additional training is also available for those who have a heart to serve as a first responder to women in their church. Care Net has recently launched a DVD training curriculum designed to equip God's Church to offer compassion, hope and help to anyone in who is considering abortion.

As you consider how God is calling you to engage on the life issue, there are many options to consider. You can begin your journey by calling [4] your local center and discussing service opportunities. It's likely that you will be an answer to the center's prayers. Or, if you are called to serve within your own church, consider Care Net's church training. Whichever direction you take, the most important thing to remember is that God is faithful. He will lead, equip and sustain you. So, like my friend Catherine, you can put

---

4   To find a center near you, visit *care-net.org/find-a-pregnancy-center*

fear aside, trust in God as you follow his voice and be assured, if God is calling, your journey will be amazing.

"Trust in the LORD with all your heart, and do not lean on your own understanding. In all your ways acknowledge him, and he will make straight your paths." (Prov. 3:5-6).

FIFTEEN

INSIGHTS INTO THE PRO-LIFE MOVEMENT

A ROUNDTABLE DISCUSSION WITH JEANNE MANCINI, KELLY ROSATI, CINDY HOPKINS, CHARMAINE YOEST

BY LINDSAY SWARTZ

The most vulnerable members of our society have been exploited for years by those who are responsible for their protection. Unborn little girls and little boys have, for too long, been the victims of our society of choice. And they aren't the only casualties. As pro-choice advocates purport, there is a war on women, but not in the way our pro-choice friends would lead us to believe. We've asked four female pro-life leaders with many years of experience to speak to the real war on women and what we, as Christians, can do about it.

* * *

Jeanne Mancini is the President of the March for Life Education and Defense Fund.

Kelly Rosati is the Vice President of Community Outreach at Focus on the Family where she oversees the Adoption & Orphan Care Initiative and the Sanctity of Human Life department.

Cindy Hopkins is the Vice President of Center Services & Client Care at Care Net.

Charmaine Yoest is President and CEO of Americans United for Life (AUL), the legal architects of the pro-life movement.

* * *

The pro-life movement is often framed in the media as a war on women. As female, Christian, pro-life leaders, what is your response to this charge?

JM: Nothing could be further from the truth. The real war that many women are battling is confusing messages about their vocation and identity (for example, to be pro-woman one must be pro-choice). Being pro-life is about embracing an authentic understanding of the human person and the beauty of the dignity and vocation of a woman. A woman's capacity to be a mother is inherent; it is part of her God-given nature. Regardless of if she becomes a mother biologically, it is wrong to try to separate that incredible aspect from who she is as a person.

CH: When I think of pro-life people interacting with women who are considering abortion, I think of compassion, hope and help. I believe the real assault on women takes place when they are told abortion is an easy answer to their complicated problems; when they are not given opportunity to explore realistic alternatives to abortion, including single parenting, adoption and marriage. Ironically, the real war on women is lived out every day in abortion clinics across our nation—places where carnage and casualties are the norm.

CY: The abortion industry wages a true war on women and the children they carry. This money-hungry industry is fundamentally a business. These profiteers in human misery show great gall in telling people that they are somehow victims of "war" when they are profiting from women's pain.

KR: Our movement is passionately pro-woman and pro-child. We reject the false premise that pits the interests of women against the interests of children. And as Christians, we follow the One who radically demonstrated the value of both.

Often forgotten in the credo of "a woman's right to choose" is the damage done to women by the abortion industry. Can you speak to this?

CH: I have been talking to women about abortion for more than 25 years and have heard their stories of pain and seen their lives affected by immense sorrow. There have been a lot of voices on social media lately trying to normalize and destigmatize abortion by saying it is "no big deal." I do believe that, for some women, the emotional pain is so deep that stuffing it down deep is easier than dealing with the painful reality of the abortion choice.

CY: What's interesting about a "right to choose" is that big abortion wants women to choose without having all the facts. Anyone who has a medical procedure knows that you are given detailed information to read, and then you have to schedule your procedure and a follow-up appointment. But with abortion surgery, the abortion industry offers little information and no follow-up care.

You can learn more detail about the health risks of abortion for women at aul.org, but approximately 10 percent of women will suffer complications from abortions, and about one in 50 women will face complications that can be life-threatening. The risk of suicide is three times greater for a woman who aborted her child compared to the woman who delivered her child. And sadly, 10 percent of mental health problems women suffer can be directly linked to abortion.

JM: Abortion is never good for women. In addition to taking the life of a precious child, abortion hurts women, psychologically and physically. Many studies have revealed this sad reality. That's why, as Christians, we must always share the message of hope and healing in Christ when addressing the topic of abortion.

One of the other charges by the pro-choice lobby is that to be pro-life is to care only for the baby up until the moment of birth.

Planned Parenthood claims to offer needed services (beside abortion) to women in crisis. How can the pro-life community address these concerns?

CY: Under Cecile Richards' leadership, life-saving health care has been cut, while Planned Parenthood's abortion business went up, even while the overall number of abortions declined. In fact, far from emphasizing health care, Planned Parenthood decreed that as of January 2013, *all* of its affiliates must perform abortions. In contrast to its growing abortion business, during the era of mega-center expansion, Planned Parenthood's overall client base has declined by 10 percent. Simultaneously, cancer screening and prevention services have been cut by more than 50 percent.

JM: The reality of the situation is that our country is home to well over 2,000 pregnancy care centers, which provide such resources to women who have chosen life. These resources include clothing, shelter, counseling, medical testing, baby diapers, formulas, cribs, etc. Compare this to the approximately 700 abortion clinics.

KR: Some of the preventive health services that Planned Parenthood provides are important for women. But under no circumstances should the government finance those important preventive health care services through an organization that destroys pre-born life. That's why community health centers, federally qualified health clinics and, in particular, the Christian community health center movement are so important.

It's also crucial to care for the children after they're born, and we have more work to do. The Christian community has led the way on this front in so many ways, but many modern day orphans in foster care—more than 100,000—are still waiting for adoptive families to come for them. With more than 300,000 churches in the United States, we ought to do better by these children. Can you imagine the power of the Christian pro-life witness if there were no more kids in foster care waiting for adoptive families?

CH: James 1:27 reminds us that religion that God accepts as pure and faultless is about looking after orphans and widows. In today's culture, a widow is a woman without a husband, and an orphan is a child without a father. Since 85 percent of the more than one million women who have abortions in the U.S. every year are unmarried, our society is replete with cultural widows and orphans. In light of the church's mandate to minister to this demographic, I believe the church is the solution to our abortion culture.

How important are the series of undercover Planned Parenthood videos to the pro-life cause?

JM: The Center for Medical Progress videos focus public attention on Planned Parenthood. They also provide a startling snapshot of the abortion industry and raise legal questions. Several states have defunded Planned Parenthood since the videos began to be released, with more investigating that possibility. The videos also offer an opportunity to dialogue about life and human dignity with those who normally are not open to having such conversations.

KR: I think they are significant but not as significant as they should be. Unfortunately, the impact wasn't what we would logically expect from the horrific revelations. What we need is spiritual, and continued prayer and perseverance is necessary. We have to maintain our hope in Jesus as we continue in the cause.

CH: While the video content is ugly and evil, we can trust that God will use them to change hearts and minds. In fact, more than 65,000 people participated in an August (2015) protest in front of Planned Parenthood facilities across our country. As attention mounts and investigations continue, we can be hopeful that the exposing light of truth will overshadow and destroy the darkness of abortion.

CY: The abortion industry has hidden behind words like "war on women" and "choice" to camouflage the deadly truth of what goes on behind closed doors. But the videos have breathed life into the debate because the facts are these: abortion ends lives, which the abortion industry treats as a product and with contempt for human dignity. The abortion industry doesn't care about women; it cares about money. Most importantly, the videos have illustrated a fundamental truth our culture has wanted to avoid: Planned Parenthood is harvesting baby parts because they do have value—and that monetary value is rooted in the fact that those babies are human.

What are some of the most helpful and practical ways that Christians can be an advocate for life in their communities?

JM: There are possibilities that range from coordinating a small pro-life group at your church, to writing pro-life opinion pieces for your local newspaper, to staying educated on current events as they relate to life issues, to praying in front of clinics, volunteering at a pregnancy care center, attending the March for Life and last, but not least, financially supporting a pro-life organization to enable its particular work.

KR: Support your local pregnancy resource center or pregnancy medical clinic. Pray for the staff, their clients, and the babies whose lives are in jeopardy. Pray for those involved in the abortion movement, for their eyes to be opened and their hearts converted to Christ. Being truly pro-life means understanding the dignity and value of every single human life, being a conduit for the extravagant love of God for every person and being willing to speak up for those who can't speak for themselves.

CH: Christians can recognize that even if they have never had an abortion, they can be a voice of influence to someone who thinks abortion is their only option. Volunteering at a pregnancy center is worth exploring. Care Net can help you find one near you. Also, educating yourself on how to talk to someone who is facing a pregnancy decision is important because words matter. Telling a friend that abortion is sin and murder, while true, is not likely change her mind. Instead, you could tell her that you are glad she told you, she's not alone and you will walk with her. Never be afraid to say abortion is wrong, but say it with a hefty dose of compassion.

CY: Carefully reading this chapter is a great start. Become informed and get involved. At Americans United for Life, we work on legislation and political issues, and we'd love to have you join our

#TeamLife, which is a way of engaging with policy. We also partner with 40 Days for Life, which is a prayer ministry.

Can you point us to some of the most helpful pro-life resources?

JM: Two of my favorite general pro-life resources were written in part by former colleague, Cathy Ruse—*Top Ten Myths of Abortion* and *The Best Pro-Life Arguments for Secular Audiences*. Some of my favorite go-to organizations for pro-life information are the Charlotte Lozier Institute, Americans United for Life, and Family Research Council.

KR: At Focus on the Family, we have pro-life resources to help you be a voice for life in your church, community, school and family. Most are downloadable and available at beavoice.net. Also, Randy Alcorn's book *Pro-Life Answers to Pro-Choice Questions* is a classic.

CH: Care Net has a tremendous resource titled, *Before You Decide*, designed for millennials considering abortion. We have a companion piece for men called *Before She Decides*. I am also excited that in early 2016 Care Net will be launching a video-based training curriculum to equip church members to provide for the needs of women who are brave enough to say "no" to abortion.

* * *

The fight to see the sanctity of life upheld, even in the most hidden places of our society, calls for endurance. It's not for the fainthearted or the weary. But neither is the call of our Lord to lay down our lives, take up our crosses and follow him. So, let's follow him into the pregnancy care centers, into the troubled teen's life, onto the front steps of the abortion clinic, into the voting booths, and into the daily monotony of changing diapers and wiping noses in order to see the gospel proclaimed, lives transformed, babies born and souls saved.

SIXTEEN

LIVING OUT PRO-LIFE CONVICTIONS

BY BETSY CHILDS HOWARD

I am a child of the 80s. My Christian parents took me to pro-life marches, and we had a bumper sticker that said, "Abortion stops a beating heart." But then things quieted down. In spite of all the activism and rallies, not much changed. One Christian woman of my parents' generation told me, "I think after the 80s and 90s passed with no change in laws, my generation got complacent and threw our hands up."

As I grew into adulthood, I felt uneasy about the quiet, not just in the public square, but in my own heart. I knew in my head that abortion was wrong, but I found it hard to care about. It was out of sight and out of mind. Sometimes I would pray, "Lord, help me to care about the sin of abortion."

It took a while for God to answer that prayer, but he did. In my mid-20s, I moved into an urban neighborhood. My apartment was just around the corner from the local Planned Parenthood. I felt weighed down by the knowledge that lives were being ended every week, just a stone's throw from my home.

I was haunted by a question that I could imagine future generations, perhaps my grandchildren, asking me, "Why didn't you do anything?" This is the question we ask of ordinary Germans who lived in the shadow of Nazi concentration camps. Some have defended themselves by saying they didn't know what was happening, but we respond that they should have known. Perhaps they didn't want to know. Now I was living in the shadow of an abortion clinic, and I knew what was happening there. Reluctantly, I decided that I could no longer pretend it wasn't happening.

GETTING INVOLVED IN THE PRO-LIFE MOVEMENT

I found my way in through a movement called 40 Days for Life. Each spring and fall, local chapters of 40 Days for Life hold peaceful vigils outside abortion clinics for 40 days. Anyone can sign up for a one-hour timeslot, with the goal of a constant presence in front of the clinics. Prayer is the main focus, but some volunteers also counsel women who want to talk, though they never shout at them or harass them.

I felt foolish and unsophisticated at first, standing on that sidewalk amongst the other volunteers with pro-life signs that hadn't changed much since those marches in the 80s. I felt conspicuous as cars drove by. But the women sitting in their cars waiting for the clinic to open felt conspicuous too, and after a while my focus shifted to them. I knew enough about the after effects of abortion to know that most of those women would never be the same.

Some women were teary, others cavalier. Most wore baggy sweatshirts, and none of them wanted to make eye contact with us. Occasionally, a husband or boyfriend would talk to us and tell us he wanted the baby but that there was nothing he could do to stop the abortion. Still more common was the man who dropped a woman off, leaving her to face the abortion alone.

When it came to talking to the women, I felt torn. Would telling them that they were about to kill a living human being—their own child—simply compound their guilt and shame after they had done it? I decided that the chance to keep them from ruining their lives (and ending the life of their unborn children) was worth it, though I chose my words carefully. Often, if I said anything, it would be, "You don't have to do this. We will help you." I wondered if any of those women had woken up that morning praying for a way out, and I wanted to offer them one.

I felt bolder with the parents, grandparents and boyfriends I talked to. "She is never going to be the same after this," I would say. "She's going to suffer. And when she does, come back to us, and we will try to help her through it."

YOU CAN MAKE A DIFFERENCE

I would love to see *Roe vs. Wade* overturned, but until it is, we can make a difference one life at a time. Women do change their minds. During every 40 Days for Life campaign, someone would drive past our sidewalk to introduce us to a toddler or child, safely buckled into a car seat. They would tell us that in a previous year, they had an appointment at the clinic, but when they saw us on the sidewalk, they couldn't go through with it.

Even if you never say a word out loud, your presence in front of a clinic may save a baby's life.

We especially need to see more mothers of young children out on the sidewalk in front of abortion clinics. Unlike many ministry opportunities, you don't need childcare to pray in front of a clinic. Your children actually enhance your ministry there by reminding women what the child in their womb will grow to be. I recommend sidewalk chalk for occupying kids while you pray. Their drawings will leave behind a reminder of the sweetness of childhood.

There are many other ways to become active as a pro-life woman; you could volunteer at a crisis pregnancy center or become a foster or adoptive mother. You can vote for pro-life candidates at the state and national level, or even consider running for office yourself. You can give money to organizations committed to ending abortion, such as And Then There Were None (abortionworker.com), a ministry that helps abortion workers leave the industry and find other jobs or the Psalm 139 Project (psalm139project.org), which provides ultrasound machines to crisis pregnancy centers.

In addition to these possibilities, I urge you not to overlook the ministries of prayer and presence. The fight to end abortion is not just a political, economic or medical fight. It is a spiritual battle. As you pray about how to get involved on behalf of the unborn, here are some suggestions of first steps you can take:

- Go with a friend or family member to pray in front of an abortion clinic. It's unwise to enter this spiritual battleground alone.

- Have contact information for a crisis pregnancy center with you. Even better, pick up some brochures that you could give to patients who may be open to changing their mind. Know the hours and location so that if a woman wants to leave the clinic and go to a crisis pregnancy center, she can follow you there.
- Find a 40 Days for Life chapter near you at 40daysforlife.com. You can sign up for a time slot to pray in front of a clinic. Consider speaking to your church leaders about whether your church could commit to covering a whole day with prayer volunteers.
- Bring your Bible! If you don't know what to pray, read through the Psalms, asking the mighty God of Israel to defeat and tear down the stronghold of abortion.
- Go in hope that God has raised you up as his warrior to fight for the lives of the unborn and the hearts of their mothers.

SEVENTEEN

PRO·LIFE ON CAMPUS

A TESTIMONY

BY KRISSIE INSERRA

In 2002, I found myself in an all-day training session to become a peer counselor at my local crisis pregnancy center. Looking back, I honestly have no idea how I even knew about the opportunity. Perhaps I heard something about it from my church or by word of mouth, but I was there, listening. As I listened to all the possible scenarios the center finds itself ministering in and heard about the immense need for caring and compassionate counselors, something clicked. This was my calling! I was getting a minor in psychology, after all, so of course my 21-year-old self thought that made me an expert on all things counseling. I knew this was what I was meant to do.

Because I was in college, I was assigned to the moms and babies room, where material assistance is provided for mothers who have chosen life for their babies. Every Thursday night, I would go up the stairs above a little Italian restaurant in a Winn-Dixie shopping center and spend two hours volunteering. I would fold baby clothes, read pamphlets and articles, and spend time getting to know these precious pregnant moms. I had so much to learn.

I wasn't quite the counseling gem that I had imagined myself to be. One client was making conversation and asked if I had any children. My reply was, "Oh, no, of course not. I'm still in college and I'm not even married!" She was also in college and not married. Open mouth, insert foot. She took my comment with grace, but I still shudder when I think about it. Clearly, God had much to teach me about ministering to the vulnerable.

About a year passed, and I had to leave Tallahassee and the center that I had grown to love. I was getting married, and we were moving to Kentucky for my husband to go to seminary. Life got busy there, and I immediately began working and never gave the pregnancy center much thought. A year and a half later, we wound up back in Tallahassee for my husband to take a job in ministry. I was still working full time and within a few months, we were pregnant with our first child. It was an incredible surprise because we had reason to believe that pregnancy would not come easy for us. Our son was born with what we understood to be major complications, so that took all our time and energy. Again, no thought was given to the pregnancy center.

As we saw God's miraculous healing hand over our son's life, we decided to try to have another baby. This was the proof of what we initially thought: getting pregnant was no simple task. While I was in the phase of begging God for another baby, it seemed that everyone around me was getting pregnant effortlessly. I started remembering my time at the pregnancy center and began to feel angry. Here I was, trying to follow Jesus with all my heart, and yet there was this incredible longing that wasn't being fulfilled.

Meanwhile, there were countless women who found themselves with an "unwanted" pregnancy, just willing to throw it all away for the sake of convenience. My heart ached for those babies. I would have adopted any one of them in a heartbeat. It was around that time that my pro-life passion began to actually develop. I was provoked by the ever-increasing pro-abortion culture. Something needed to be done.

In God's perfect timing, we had another son. We were overjoyed to bring another baby boy into our family. This time, he was healthy, and life as we knew it seemed perfect.

About a year and a half later, my husband, Dean, called me as I was dropping our oldest off at preschool and started the conversation with, "Okay, before you say no, I just need you to hear me out." Great opener. I was totally skeptical, but listening.

He had just attended an annual pastoral prayer summit at the same pregnancy center where I had volunteered in college and met the new director. He was with a couple of other local pastors for that hour and was handed a prayer guide with a specific prayer request assigned to each person. His assignment was to pray for the right person to be hired in the brand new position as the Campus Coordinator for the center.

The pregnancy center is strategically located on the campus of Florida State University and is minutes from two other colleges and universities as well. So, there are roughly 75,000 college students within a three to five mile radius. With a small staff of five women, they needed someone to focus on marketing to those students. That year, there were over 2,000 reported pregnancies at Florida State alone. Dean prayed over this petition, and when he was finished, he looked at the director and said, "I have your campus coordinator . . . my wife." It was the fastest prayer request answer of all time.

This was not on my radar by any stretch of the imagination. After all, I had two young boys at home, and Dean was the pastor of a rapidly growing church plant. I felt compelled to minister to these pregnant women and their babies whose lives hung in the balance. I knew that roughly 10 percent of college students each year are involved in an unplanned pregnancy. I knew that around 25 percent of women ages 20-24 have had abortions. I may not be great at math, but I know that's a staggering number of babies in my city, just a few miles from my house, who are never given a chance to take their first breath. These babies are no different from my own little boys, and this "cause" became very *personal*.

Suddenly, I felt an incredible urgency to join in with this amazing group of ladies and take this monster of abortion head-on. As I rolled up my sleeves and got to work, I quickly realized that it was not enough for my compassion to simply be for the babies. I was trained (again) to counsel women in a crisis pregnancy situation so that I could take walk-in clients while in the office. God began to do an incredible work in my heart. Instead of being angry with these mothers for even considering ending the life of their child, I began to truly hear their stories and see the paralyzing fear that had overcome them. Sure, many had made a series of poor choices that led them to this counseling room, but I was quickly able to see Satan's lies that had them trapped—lies and deception, such as, "You have your whole life ahead of you. If you have this baby, it will all be over. You'll have to drop out of school. Your parents will stop supporting you financially. Your boyfriend will leave. You will be all alone with no support." They got deeper and more cutting: "If God is good, how did he let this happen? He will never accept you now. You've already had an abortion in the past; God cannot forgive you for that, so you might as well solve your new problem, too." I saw these women, and my heart melted. I was seeing them as Jesus sees them, "harassed and helpless, like sheep without a shepherd" (Matt. 9:36).

Our mission was not merely to go into the counseling room and change the mother's mind about her pregnancy. We certainly did see that happen many times, but this ministry was bigger than an ultrasound room where the women could get a glimpse into the window of their wombs and see their squirming, very much alive baby, and choose life.

Thankfully the choice for life happens often, as roughly 80 percent of women who see their baby through an ultrasound choose to carry their child. Our greatest reason for existence as a pregnancy center was to tell these women and men (we see fathers, too!) about the incredible saving love of Jesus Christ and to show them that he actively pursues them in grace.

To this day, I almost never see a client without sharing the gospel of Jesus Christ and explaining why he is their hope in this present situation. I have grown so much from the self-assured college student a decade before. I learned very quickly to pray earnestly each time I entered the counseling room and to remain in prayer during the entire conversation. I have cried with my hurting clients and rejoiced with those who were rescued from the pits of hell by hearing the gospel story. I often wonder if it's more of a blessing for me than for the client.

I recently had lunch with a friend who wanted to talk about "pro-life issues." When we sat down, she got right to the heart of the matter. Like so many others, she had always been supportive of life in the womb but went about her day-to-day business and kind of forgot about the true death chambers that were present in the abortion clinics of our town—that is, until the series of undercover videos came out exposing some of the heinous practices of Planned Parenthood. "I just can't turn my head away anymore. I have to do something!" she said. I encouraged her to get involved with our pregnancy center, whether it was in counselling, office work, a daily prayer team, or even do yard work on weekends at the center. That evening, she attended the fundraising banquet for the center and committed to getting involved. It was that simple. The issue had become *personal* to her.

Sometimes the motivation to be involved in the pro-life movement evolves over time, like it did with me. However, sometimes it's in a moment where you decide you simply can't look away any longer. Either way, they are just good intentions until you do something. Find a local pregnancy help center that is not only helping women and men to see the truth about the life that God created inside of them, but one that is also drawing them to know and follow that Creator himself. When, by God's grace, they receive eternal life, choosing life becomes *personal* to them.

EIGHTEEN

CONCLUSION

BY TRILLIA NEWBELL

Tamara* grew up in a loving home with two parents. People who knew her would have said she was an overachiever, one of those "Most Likely to Succeed" types. She was one of the many African-Americans in her high school to receive scholarships to attend college. Then she met an older man who stole her heart and her virginity.

Pregnant at 18, she made the choice to have an abortion. Unfortunately, Tamara remained in sin, and by the time she was in her mid-20s, she had undergone four more abortions. Now 30 years old with two kids, Tamara lives with an ache in her heart at the unnecessary loss of the other children through her choice to abort them.

"Having children made me realize the ultimate value of life beyond my selfish motivations of what I felt life was about," Tamara told me. "After having my first child, I realized or began to feel that the other children I once had the opportunity to have were still my children. I have dealt with a greater sense of regret and conviction after having children. I have realized the gift it is to be chosen by God to nurture and raise the seeds he plants, his children, whether they were conceived by sin and lust or by love."

She made the decisions to abort to "save a relationship [with her boyfriend] for four of them and the fifth due to finances and fear." Tamara now believes that abortion is wrong.

"It is a weird thing, abortion. It is wrong in the sense that someone would even have the idea to create such a procedure to begin with. It is wrong to think that someone wouldn't take responsibility for their actions. It is wrong that young men don't understand the effect it has on the young woman or girl who lies in the cold, cold, cold room with a group of other women to ultimately remove a child as if it is a parasite. It's heavy," she shared through tears.

Tamara is now on a journey to understand God's forgiveness of sins through Christ's sacrificial death on the cross.

"I repeatedly decided to have abortions because I wasn't serving the good will of my Lord. I was blindly living in the world and serving people and relationships, dreams that weren't ever fully met anyway due to conviction and self-doubt. I still have a looming feeling of guilt from time to time and am still on a journey to understand God's love for me and Christ's sacrifice for these sins I have committed."

NO SIN TOO GREAT

A recent LifeWay Research study sponsored by Care Net showed that more than four in 10 women who have had an abortion attended church when they ended their pregnancy. Those results may be shocking to some, but given the enormous amount of abortions occurring each year in our country, it doesn't seem implausible. What grieves me, along with the loss of life, is the apparent fear and silence of those who are considering abortions. The study shows that only seven percent of women discussed their abortion decision with anyone at church and 76 percent say the church had no influence on their decision to terminate a pregnancy. Only one percent reported that someone from their local church influenced their decision while 38 percent said the father had some influence. These are sobering statistics—perhaps most for what it reveals about the culture of our churches.

As reported by the Baptist Press: Only 38 percent of women who have had an abortion consider church a safe place to discuss pregnancy options including parenting, abortion and adoption. And while 25 percent say they would recommend a friend or family member discuss an unplanned pregnancy with someone at church, more than twice as many (54 percent) say they would not recommend it.[1]

The troubling study shows a culture of silence among women who are afraid of being shamed or gossiped about. We want and need our churches to be places where men and women can share openly and honestly about their struggles. The results of this research do not surprise me, but they do grieve me. My hope is that the gospel of grace would break through a culture of fear and gossip so that women may be served well. We must be equipped on how to properly handle these tough circumstances with truth covered in gentleness and love.

If you are among the thousands of women who have chosen to abort your child, I want to share God's grace with you. John Piper

---

1   http://bpnews.net/45893/abortion-womens-views-of-church-focus-of-study

has helpfully and powerfully addressed the topic abortion as it relates to race. Hear this word for you:

> And lest anyone think that you are simply too sinful—that there have been too many sins for too long—listen to the way the great sinner, the apostle Paul, speaks to you—directly to you. This is 1 Timothy 1:15-16: "Christ Jesus came into the world to save sinners, of whom I am the foremost. But I received mercy for this reason, that in me, as the foremost, Jesus Christ might display his perfect patience as an example to those who were to believe in him for eternal life." In other words, if God can save me, the foremost (he was a murdering Christian-hater), then he can save anyone who comes to him. "Everyone who calls on the name of the Lord will be saved" (Rom. 10:13).[2]

There is forgiveness in Christ. If you are convicted of your sin, confess it and ask God to forgive you. Then walk in that forgiveness in the light (Eph. 5:8-11), and speak with a pastor or Christian counselor to assist you further.

Women on Life covered much of the real-life circumstances women like Tamara will face. As you know, the value and dignity of life goes beyond the unborn, though the unborn shouldn't be minimized or overlooked as a result. Due to the scope of the book, we did not cover sex-trafficking, but consider how even that would be affected if our churches began to discuss these topics openly and honestly, covered with grace and love. The gospel reaches into the darkest and hardest stories and brings life and light. We have

---

2   John Piper, *Desiring God*, January 21, 2007. http://www.desiringgod.org/messages/when-is-abortion-racism.

a hope that endures forever and a King who was tempted in every way but without sin. Let's change the culture and climate of our churches so that all of life can be addressed without fear.

* * *

Tamara is not the interviewee's real name. Her first and last name has been concealed to protect the identity of her children and the men involved in the circumstances above.

LELAND
HOUSE
PRESS

Leland House Press is an initiative from The Ethics and
Religious Liberty Commission. Leland House Press exists
to equip and educate the local church about ethical and
religious liberty issues through the publication of various
eBooks and booklets.

For more information about Leland House Press and the
latest titles, visit **erlc.com/leland**

Made in the USA
San Bernardino, CA
15 February 2018